TWO TRUTHS AND A LIE

TWO
AND A

TRUTHS
LIE

Histories
and
Mysteries

AMMI-JOAN PAQUETTE
and LAURIE ANN THOMPSON

WALDEN POND PRESS
An Imprint of HarperCollinsPublishers

Walden Pond Press is an imprint of HarperCollins Publishers.
Walden Pond Press and the skipping stone logo are trademarks and registered trademarks of
Walden Media, LLC.

Two Truths and a Lie: Histories and Mysteries
Text copyright © 2018 by Ammi-Joan Paquette and Laurie Ann Thompson
Illustrations copyright © 2018 by Lisa K. Weber
www.harpercollinschildrens.com
ISBN 978-0-06-241886-9
Typography by Aurora Parlagreco
18 19 20 21 22 SCP 10 9 8 7 6 5 4 3 2 1

First Edition

To readers everywhere: stay curious . . . and skeptical

CONTENTS

INTRODUCTION

You've probably heard the saying "You can't believe everything you read." Well, when it comes to this book, you *really* can't!

Everybody knows that fiction is a made-up story that comes from someone's imagination, while nonfiction is about things that are factual and true. *This* book, however, is part nonfiction and part fiction. So, depending on how you look at it, it's both . . . or it's neither.

The world is an interesting place. Sometimes truth really *is* stranger than fiction, and sometimes fiction is so easy to believe that we don't know it's not true. As a reader, it can be hard to tell the difference. But it's important to try, and it can also be a whole lot of fun! Here's how we're going to do it.

Each part of this book has three chapters, and each chapter contains three stories. As you can probably guess from the book's title, every single chapter has:

- **Two** stories that are 100% factual TRUTHS; and

- **one** that is a made-up piece of fiction—a LIE!

But which is which? You'll have to figure *that* out for yourself!

Read each story carefully and compare it to what you already know to be true. Discuss the stories with friends, family, or teachers. Do your own research by digging around online (safely, of course!), heading to your public or school library, or asking a teacher or other adult for help. Don't be shy: asking questions is the best way to learn!

Your job won't be easy. All of the stories in this book are pretty unbelievable, but some of them are actually untrue as well. So, please be careful! In this book especially, you can't believe everything you read . . . but at least you can't say we didn't warn you.

Good luck!

PART 1
HAZY HISTORIES

History. Some people think of it as nothing more than a whole bunch of names and events and dates to be memorized. But history is so much more than that. History is people, history is stories, history is *fascinating*!

In this section, we'll spin some amazing tales, from ancient history right up to the present day. All of them are remarkable, but remember—one of the stories in each chapter is a fake.

Prepare to experience history in a way that you never have before.

Let's get started!

A. MAMMOTH CAVE'S MYSTERY WALKER

Come walk with me, will you? Just take these few steps down—down—*down*—into the deep, dark caves. Okay, it's more than *a few* steps. Nestled several hundred feet below Kentucky hill country, Mammoth Cave is the longest cave system in the world, with over 400 miles of

Do you dare brave the cave?!

mapped passages. That's as wide as the whole country of Germany, or about the driving distance between Los Angeles and San Francisco. It would take a brisk walker 100 hours to go from start to finish—or four days at a nonstop clip! (Spoiler alert: it's far.)

Between you and me and the bat **guano**, though, Mammoth Cave is absolutely worth the trip. Lucky visitors descend 280 steps into the dank, chilly underearth, where stalactites coat the ceiling and stalagmites grow along the ground and every wall drips a chilly invitation. But the coolest thing about Mammoth Cave is not its length, nor its brisk mid-50s temperature, nor even the many creepy tales and legends that pack its history. (Look 'em up!)

The coolest thing of all can be found in an enormous room called the Mirror Walk Way. It's a long, narrow passage that winds on a thin peak, so visitors walk through in single file with a breathtaking drop to either side. At the midway point comes the corker. Stop in the center. Now, look up. The ceiling is a good thirty feet above, with subtly installed light showing off the various **formations**. And there, clearly visible on its limestone surface, is a footprint. In fact, it's the first in a long string of footprints, which make their eerie way along

the ceiling—exactly mirroring the path of the winding walk below!

Because of the height of the ceiling and **precariousness** of the trail, a full testing has yet to be done on the marks. But a few things have been learned already: The prints are *ancient*—at least 3,000 years old, if not more. They are gouged deep into the stone, in the shape of bare feet—so clearly that each toe can be seen on well over half of the prints. They follow a ceiling route that matches the trail below—before stopping abruptly right in front of a deep hollow basin leading up through the ceiling.

And there's one more thing: each print is no more than four inches long. In other words? The upside-down stone walker was very likely *a kid*!

The so-called Mystery Walker has been baffling **speleologists** for decades. Could the clearly visible footprints—formed in solid stone, no less!—have been made by real feet, and the stone walls shifted over time so that what was below somehow came to be above?

Or could the marks have actually been caused by some volatile mix of the

abundant sulfur, gypsum, and saltpeter that can be found in the caves? These and other questions are part of an ongoing body of research that, when answered, should shed light not only on this unknown kid of an ancient era, but perhaps also give a clear glimpse of a culture beyond the history pages.

I mean, if you had the chance to run along the ceiling deep in the Mammoth Cave, wouldn't you?

Talk It Out: What's Your Obsession?

Okay, so maybe *obsession* is a bit of a strong word. Call it "fascination" or "curiosity" or "passion"; we all have things that make us drop whatever else we're doing and pay attention. One of your trusty authors (we're not telling who!) feels that way about caves. What's not to love? Dark, mysterious, a little creepy—endlessly fascinating. Passion is like a fire that sparks inside your chest and makes everything brighter, more interesting. And the coolest thing about passion? It can turn into a lifelong treasure hunt as you learn more and more about your favorite things.

So . . . what about you? What makes your eyes widen and your stomach clench? What do you want to learn about, or know about, or do, more than anything else in the world? Why? It's worth thinking about—and then sharing those thoughts with others! And it's also worth following up with action: research, exploration, study, play, list-making, reading, talking to people. Who knows where your passion might lead?

B. HOLEY MOLARS!

Have you ever had a **cavity** in one of your teeth and gone to the dentist to get a filling? If so, it probably wasn't one of your favorite experiences of all time. But, can you imagine what it must have been like to go to the dentist more than 10,000 years ago? Let's just say that people back then had it a whole lot worse than we do today!

Modern dentists can choose from an array of painkillers to make dental work more tolerable for their patients. They use specialized tools so their work is fast and efficient. They have a variety of advanced materials available to make their repairs safe and durable. Plus, they can usually detect cavities when they are

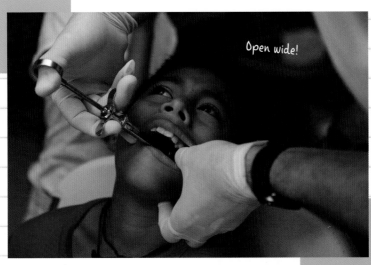

Open wide!

still small and easy to fix. This all makes it fairly easy for dentists to help us keep our teeth healthy and strong.

Even with our modern dental hygiene and extensive knowledge about how to prevent cavities, they still remain one of the most common dental problems around the world today. And, unfortunately, that's nothing new. While prehistoric dentists did not have the advantages your dentist does today, people back then still needed dental work. After all, it's hard to eat when you have a terrible toothache, and the infection can be dangerous if left untreated. So, cavities should definitely be fixed . . . somehow.

A tooth found in Italy shows that one early dentist was already "drilling" holes to remove cavities approximately 14,000 years ago, a time when humans were still mostly hunter-gatherers. Researchers have concluded that sharp flint tools were used to scratch and pry at the infected **molar**. Ouch! Clearing out the

This might hurt a little. . . .

cavity must've taken a very long time—and been extremely painful—for the poor patient, a man about twenty-five years old. And it appears that's where the treatment ended. The pit in the young man's molar was apparently left open, without the benefit of any kind of filling.

The oldest known examples of dental fillings were discovered later in a pair of **incisors**, also found in Italy. Researchers estimated that the teeth date back to between 12,740 and 13,000 years ago. Sophisticated analysis showed that large holes were "drilled" into them by digging and scraping at the teeth with sharpened rocks. But that was only the beginning. It also looked like the holes had been filled in with something. But what could it be?

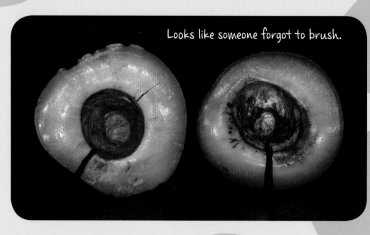

Looks like someone forgot to brush.

Samples taken from inside the pits in the teeth gave researchers some clues. Apparently, the ancient dentist used vegetable fibers and hair, all held together with a sticky substance called bitumen. Bitumen comes from oil and is now used to pave roads. If the thought of that being put into your mouth isn't disgusting enough, just imagine what it must have tasted like. Ew!

So, the next time you go to the dentist, be grateful for all of the modern advances he or she uses to take good care of your teeth. And if you do happen to get a cavity, just be happy your dentist is quite a bit more sophisticated than one practicing in the late **Upper Paleolithic era**!

Better Off Buried—Or Not!

Whether in a time capsule, treasure chest, or just lost under mounds of earth, every one of these objects was discovered buried underground. All, that is, but one! Can you guess which?

1. Mummified Ferrari sports car—California, USA (1978)

2. A woman's lost wedding ring, 16 years later, around a carrot—Sweden (2011)

3. Helmet from the Battle of Marathon in 490 BC, with warrior's skull reportedly still inside—Greece (1834)

4. Three oak doors, standing upright all in a row—Venezuela (1911)

5. Canisters containing $10 million in gold coins from the 1800s—California, USA (2014)

6. Fossilized baleen whale weighing 1,000 pounds and dating back 14 to 16 million years—California, USA (1978)

7. A 15-ton ball of fat the size of a bus—London, England (2013)

8. Dozens of fighter jets—Iraq (2003)

9. Three-masted Gold Rush-era ship known as *General Harrison*—California, USA (2001)

10. Box of keepsakes belonging to a teenage girl from AD 650—Aldeburgh, England (2013)

C. A CURSE ON ALL THIEVING BATHERS

People who lived hundreds—even thousands—of years ago might seem quite strange to us now. They often looked, spoke, and did things quite differently than we do today. So there's always a bit of a double take at that moment of discovery when we see that inhabitants of the historical past really *were* a lot like you or me—just with their own, you know, historical twist.

Take the locker room. Have you ever gone swimming in a public pool or gone to gym class, leaving your clothes and other stuff behind— only to come back and find some of it *gone?*

Poxy: Bad or generally disliked

Taken by some **poxy** thief? If you haven't, lucky you. If you have, we sympathize. On the bright side, your unhappy experience gives you something in common with the inhabitants of the ancient British city of Bath.

England in modern times. Bath is here.

Beginning in 1979, archaeologists digging in Bath made a curious discovery. They were starting to uncover dozens of weird little metallic scrolls dating clear back to the fourth century AD—with some even older! Many of the scrolls contained words written in ancient Roman letters. What could they be?

First of all, you should know something about the city of Bath. It was famous for, well, its *baths*. (Shocking, I know.) Since big cities of ancient times were crowded, noisy, and dirty, people liked to travel out to the country to "take the waters" from the natural hot springs found in the area. In Roman times, this particular bath was also **revered** as a place of worship. Bath was basically an ancient-day religious spa.

Revered: Prized or admired

But while you or I can usually tuck our valuables safely away inside lockers or stow them in the trunk of the car, ancient travelers had no such options. They had to leave their expensive clothes, money, and other stuff out in the changing room! It was a prime picking spot for thieves, who often made off with the belongings of those who visited the baths.

Left with few options, **irate** victims of this theft fought back in the best way they could: with a curse. What kind of curse, specifically? Why, a curse written on a lead tablet, of course. These were mostly written to Sulis Minerva, a warrior goddess who was supposed to keep watch over these particular hot springs. In fact, many people were there to worship her in particular. So, naturally, they called on their goddess to right their wrongs. The messages were written in various languages, and some were even in code! Here are a few choice examples.

There's poor Solinus, who had his tunic and cloak stolen:

Solinus to the goddess Sulis Minerva. I give to your divinity and majesty [my] bathing tunic and cloak. Do not allow sleep or health to him who has done me wrong, whether man or woman or whether slave or free, unless he reveals himself and brings [those] goods to your temple.

Six silver coins was a lot of money in those days, and so Annianus was rightfully upset:

Irate: Furious

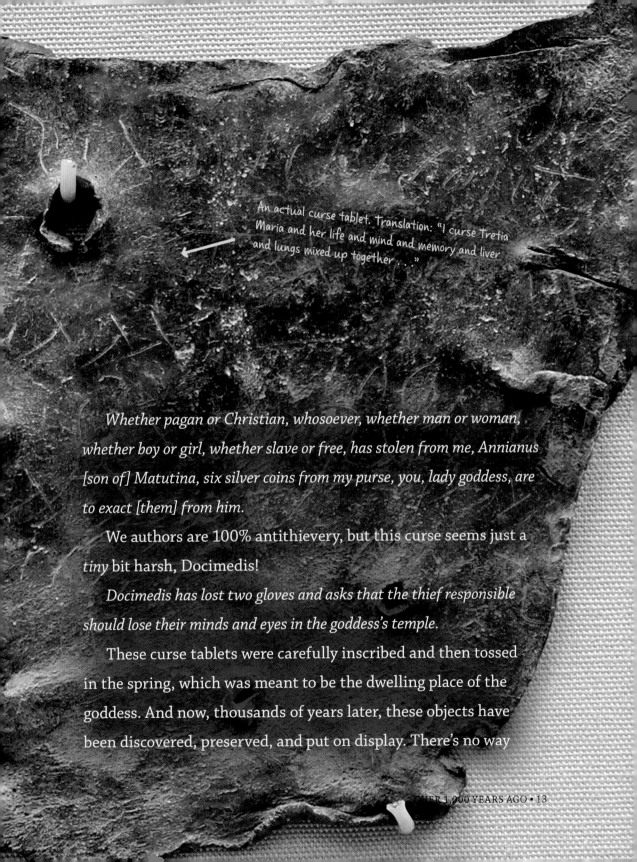

An actual curse tablet. Translation: "I curse Tretia Maria and her life and mind and memory and liver and lungs mixed up together . . ."

Whether pagan or Christian, whosoever, whether man or woman, whether boy or girl, whether slave or free, has stolen from me, Annianus [son of] Matutina, six silver coins from my purse, you, lady goddess, are to exact [them] from him.

We authors are 100% antithievery, but this curse seems just a *tiny* bit harsh, Docimedis!

Docimedis has lost two gloves and asks that the thief responsible should lose their minds and eyes in the goddess's temple.

These curse tablets were carefully inscribed and then tossed in the spring, which was meant to be the dwelling place of the goddess. And now, thousands of years later, these objects have been discovered, preserved, and put on display. There's no way of knowing what became of those people or their requests. But we can all agree that it's an interesting glimpse of the everyday lives of people who lived so long ago, yet have a surprising amount in common with us today.

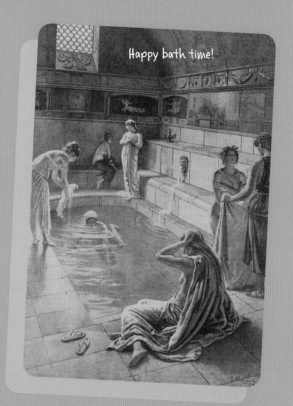

Happy bath time!

Try It: Scribe Your Own Scroll!

All thieving and cursing aside, communication in ancient times was a very different process than it is for us today. And most of us, when keeping in touch with friends and family, jump right for our phone, email, or other technological link-ups. But did you know that the post office is a pretty cool way to send messages, too—even (or especially!) ones that are a bit unconventional? Here's how you can make your own message scroll:

1. Pick a friend or relative who lives far away. Make sure you have their mailing address.

2. Get a sheet of thin, flexible cardstock. Write a letter on this sheet. Feeling creative? Draw, decorate, or otherwise embellish your missive.

3. Now get an empty tube from the inside of a roll of paper towels. Roll up your finished scroll-letter and squirrel it *inside* the cardboard tube.

4. Seal up both ends of the roll with cardstock and tape. Carefully write your friend's or relative's address on the outside of the tube. Take it to the post office for speedy delivery!

IN THIS CHAPTER, YOU *read about ancient footprints on the roof of a cave, some gruesome prehistoric dental procedures, and a creative attempt to punish opportunistic thieves. Which two can you believe? Which one is meant to trick you? First, try to guess. Then see if you can figure out if your guess is correct! And after you've done your research, check out the back of the book to see once and for all if you're right.*

CHAPTER 2

OVER 100 YEARS AGO

A. ONESIMUS AND THE FIGHT AGAINST SMALLPOX

Smallpox. The word alone used to strike terror in people across the globe, and for most of recorded history it was the deadliest disease known to humankind. **Lesions** found on the mummy of pharaoh Ramses V show that the deadly disease has plagued us for at least 3,000 years. Yet these days, we hardly hear about smallpox at all. Why? Because, fortunately, an aggressive worldwide

R.I.P. Ramses V

vaccination program in the 1960s and 1970s wiped it out. And one of the people we have to thank for that incredible feat was a man from Africa who had been kidnapped, enslaved, and brought to New England against his will.

In 1706, members of a Puritan church in Boston bought the man as a slave for

their minister, Cotton Mather. Mather named the man Onesimus after a slave referenced in the Bible. Once, when Mather asked Onesimus if he'd ever had smallpox, Onesimus gave an interesting reply. "Yes and no," he said. He showed Mather the scar on his arm and told him that, in Africa, people would take a small amount of pus from a smallpox sore on a sick person. Then they would make a small cut in a healthy person's skin and apply the smallpox pus to the fresh wound. This would give the healthy person a milder version of smallpox from which they would almost always

Cotton Mather: minister, slave owner, scientist, witch hunter

recover, Onesimus explained—*and* it would protect them from ever getting smallpox again!

Mather discovered that many other Africans in Boston had a similar scar—and that any enslaved person who bore the mark was almost always immune to the dreaded disease. Mather recognized what an important breakthrough this could be for public health in New England and beyond, vowing to try it the next time smallpox struck Boston. And he would get his chance.

Smallpox returned in 1721, and Mather was eager to try the process of **inoculation** that he had learned from Onesimus.

Inoculation: Exposure to a very small amount of a live, potent form of a disease, with the same intended effect as vaccination

Unfortunately, as terrified as people were of smallpox, most were even more distrustful of this new form of protection. Some feared it would only spread the terrible disease faster; others were simply unwilling to try anything viewed as foreign, especially

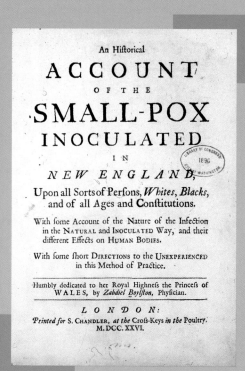

An Hiſtorical

ACCOUNT

OF THE

SMALL-POX

INOCULATED

IN

NEW ENGLAND,

Upon all Sorts of Perſons, *Whites, Blacks,* and of all Ages and **Conſtitutions.**

With ſome Account of the Nature of the Infection in the NATURAL and INOCULATED Way, and their different Effects on HUMAN BODIES.

With ſome ſhort DIRECTIONS to the UNEXPERIENCED in this Method of Practice.

Humbly dedicated to her Royal Highneſs the Princeſs of WALES, by *Zabdiel Boylſton,* Phyſician.

LONDON:

Printed for S. CHANDLER, *at the* Croſs-Keys *in the* Poultry. M. DCC. XXVI.

1726 report on the results

Try It: Be the Investigator— Does Older Mean Wiser?

It's an undeniable fact of life: people who are older have lived longer, so they have had more experience. Sometimes, along the way, they gather some pretty cool skills, too. Your mission today (should you choose to accept): Find one of those elders and ask them for their best "life hack" (a tip, technique, or remedy for an everyday problem). Bring along a notepad, or your smartphone, so you can write it down. If the remedy is something practical, useful, or interesting (oh—and also, safe!), give it a try. Who knows what amazing thing you might learn? Years ago, one of your trusty authors stopped rolling her eyes at an old uncle who always swished vinegar in his mouth whenever he burned his tongue . . . and tried it. Said author has never suffered from a burned tongue again! Honest to goodness. You, too, might end up with a secret recipe to pass down to generations to come.

African, due to their deep-seated racism. But whatever their reasons, it turned out that those who refused the new idea did so at their own peril.

Throughout the course of the epidemic, only 242 people agreed to try the new practice of inoculation. Of those, only six died, which comes out to about one in forty. When you compare that with the 844 people who died out of the 5,889 who had gotten the disease, you can see that the odds were much worse for those who weren't inoculated—about one in seven of whom perished. Clearly, the inoculations had worked.

It would still take some time before the idea of inoculating people against infectious diseases gained widespread acceptance, but the seed had been planted. In 1796, British physician Edward Jenner introduced a smallpox vaccine that was safer than the kind of direct inoculation Mather had learned from Onesimus. And finally, about 200 years later, the World Health Organization documented the last case of smallpox in the world. The scourge of smallpox had been **eradicated**, thanks in part to one man from Africa and his knowledge of inoculation.

Eradicated: Completely eliminated

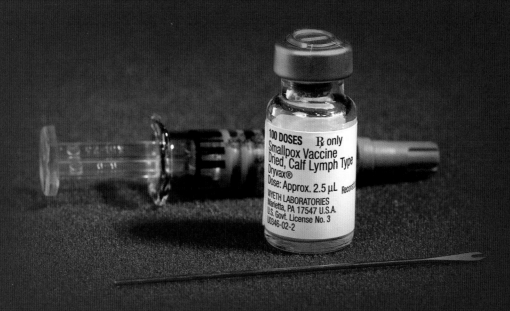

B. ALL ABOARD THE RAILWAY OF THE DEAD

//

Are you a train-savvy reader? If so, you know that if you want to go to Hogwarts, you need to go to King's Cross in London, Platform 9¾. If you want to meet Thomas the Tank Engine, you make your way to Shining Time Station. And the Polar Express might leave from a number of places, but the trip home *always* kicks off at the North Pole. But what if you wanted to ride . . . the Railway of the Dead?

For this you would need to make your way to the London Necropolis Railway (LNR) station. You would also, unfortunately, need to travel back in time. The LNR had its start in 1854,

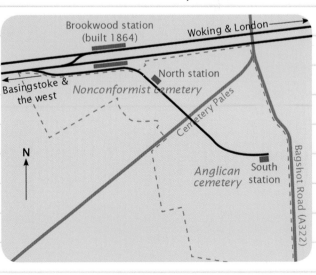

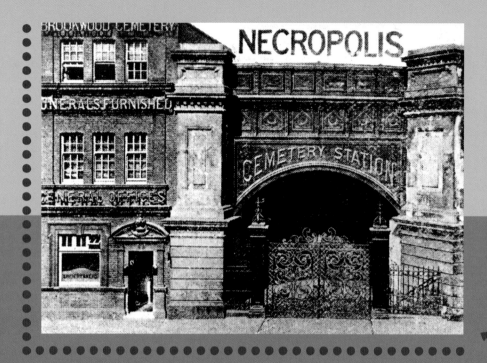

Now there's a friendly-looking train station . . .

and clear on through to 1941 it was the number one stop for every Londoner's dead body rail transport needs.

Let's set the scene a bit. London in the mid-1800s was a city bursting at the seams. Its population had more than doubled in just 50 years! More people in a city often led to more sickness—something that became particularly dangerous for Londoners in the late 1840s, when a fatal **cholera** outbreak swept through the city, leaving nearly 15,000 people dead. Graveyards were jam-packed. In some places, bodies piled up

Cholera: Highly contagious disease that causes intense vomiting and diarrhea and often leads to death

outside of churches awaiting burial. Something had to be done.

Enter that newfangled invention, the steam engine. An enterprising man named Sir Richard Broun bought a huge parcel of land 25 miles outside the city, which he proceeded to set up as a burial ground. The London Necropolis Railway was then established to provide easy transport to the cemetery—both for the bodies *and* the loved ones who would be laying them to rest.

Not everyone liked this idea. Trains had only been around for a couple of decades, after all, and many people found them terrifying. Picture it: you're not only riding this huge, scary monster machine belching out noise and smoke . . . you're also sharing the train with a bunch of dead bodies! Still, a solution is a solution, yes? So, let's take a spin along those iron tracks of progress.

Step on board, step on board! Wait— first you'll need tickets. *Two* tickets. One for you, dear mourner. And . . . one for your departed relative's coffin. Would you like a first-, second-, or third-class coffin ticket? First-class travel offers more careful handling and a more pleasing travel space. They also let you choose the burial spot in the cemetery. It's a one-way ticket for your

The official logo of the LNR!

Written in Stone

Gravestones are truly the chance to have the last word. Whether wise, weepy, or downright wacky, here are nine real-life inscriptions . . . and one that is totally fake. Can you guess which doesn't fit?

1. George Spencer Millet, age 15: "Lost life by stab in falling on ink eraser, evading six young women trying to give him birthday kisses in office Metropolitan Life Building."

2. Tomas Jimoteo Chinchilla: "Now you are in the Lord's arms. Lord, watch your wallet."

3. R. Andersen: "Connection reset by peer. He came, he saw, he logged out."

4. "Dear Departed Brother Dave: He chased a bear into a cave."

5. B. P. Roberts: "I told you I was sick."

6. Ellen Shannon: "Who was fatally burned Mar. 21, 1870 by the explosion of a lamp filled with 'R.E. Danforth's Non-Explosive Burning Fluid.'"

7. Laurel Morton: "Died as she lived: with sharpened pencil always in hand."

8. "Kay's Fudge: 2 sq. chocolate / 2 Tbs. butter / Melt on low heat. Stir in 1 cup milk. Bring to boil 3 cups sugar, 1 Tbs vanilla, pinch salt. Cook to softball stage. Pour on marble slab. Cool & beat & eat."

9. Merv Griffin: "I will <u>not</u> be right back after this message."

10. Sir Jeffrey Hudson: "A dwarf presented in a pie to King Charles 1st."

relative's coffin, but you, dear mourner, also get a return ticket. (Whew!)

And so it went. The 40-minute train ride dropped passengers and their coffin cargo at the graveyard, with a daily return trip promptly at 3:30 p.m. Enough time for a burial ceremony, swapping stories with loved ones, and perhaps a light lunch in the dappled shade or in one of the on-site refreshment buildings.

Creep factor aside, the LNR proved to be an excellent solution to a very pressing problem. According to Necropolis Railway expert John M.

Clarke, author of *The Brookwood Necropolis Railway*, during its peak the railway carried more than 2,000 dead bodies a year, for a total of about 200,000 corpses over its 87-year span of use. Finally, in 1941, the LNR sustained major damage in a World War II air raid. Repairs were determined not to be worth the expense, and the **postmortem** promenades ground to a halt.

Postmortem: After death

Still, retired or not—we reckon that's a train worth knowing about!

Mourners carrying their cargo onto the platform

C. BOILERPLATE: THE MAN, THE MYTH, THE MACHINE

//

What's the first word that comes to mind when you think about robots? "High-tech," maybe? Or "modern"? Both of those descriptions are true—*normally*. Actually, though, the roots of modern **robotics** go back a good deal further in the past than many people are aware.

Robotics: The science of designing and building robots

Conceptual: Something that's been thought of, but not yet created

A very early **conceptual** steam-powered robot was described in the works of the Greek mathematician Archytas of Tarentum in the fourth century BC, and Leonardo da Vinci drew detailed diagrams of a movable mechanical knight around 1495. Starting in the 1700s, a variety of automatons were built that were able to do all sorts of artistic and creative things—drawing

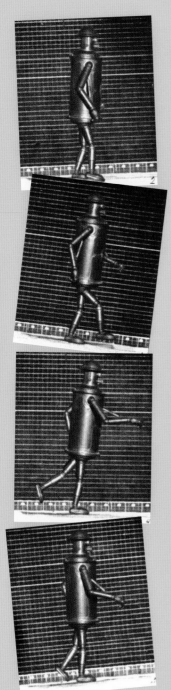

Meet Boilerplate!

and making music and more—some of them powered by steam and primitive circuits.

But—there are robots . . . and then there's Boilerplate.

Just what is Boilerplate, you may ask? I am so glad you did.

This roughly human-shaped automaton is widely considered to be the first fully independent "modern" robot. Shockingly revolutionary for its time, Boilerplate was unveiled in 1893 at the Chicago World's Fair, to widespread awe and wonder. The brainchild of the robotics genius Professor Archibald Campion, Boilerplate was originally designed as a fighting machine and programmed to do a variety of complex tasks. It was unique for its time in that those tasks could be shaped and reprogrammed according to the need and situation—a true multipurpose machine, very different from the single-task automatons that had existed up till that point.

Historians Paul Guinan and Anina Bennett have written a definitive work on the machine,

Boilerplate: History's Mechanical Marvel, which painstakingly tracks the robot's path across its years in the public eye. One of its first big successes was a trip to Antarctica, where Campion put Boilerplate's skills to the test in extreme weather and subzero temperatures. Later reports place Boilerplate as having some involvement in the Spanish-American War and the Boxer Rebellion in China. In September 1915, Boilerplate was instrumental in the recovery and raising of a sunken F-4 submarine in Hawaii at the start of World War I. This led to Boilerplate's further involvement in the war, though this was kept secret for fear of the technology falling into enemy hands.

Unfortunately, what was meant to further a grand career

With Teddy Roosevelt and the Rough Riders

ended up as this robot's last hurrah. At the height of World War I, while participating in a **classified** mission in occupied France, Boilerplate disappeared in the fall of 1918. Despite strenuous and ongoing efforts across multiple nations, no sign of the machine was ever found, nor were any significant clues as to its fate. Ironically, this disappearance only contributed to its legendary fame and launched countless conspiracy theories.

Classified: Something the government has declared to be secret

Over the centuries, Boilerplate has taken on a certain mythical, almost action-hero quality, and stories of its exploits abound across the late 1890s and into the early 1900s. Some of these stories claim an almost intelligent form of behavior. These are surely embellished, since serious artificial intelligence research did not really take off until the second half of the 1900s.

Although Boilerplate was intended as a

Talk It Out: Design Your Own Robot

If you could design and build your own robot, what features would you want it to have? How would it be powered? What would you like it to be able to do? Why? Share your thoughts with someone else, and be sure to find out theirs as well!

prototype—presumably with similar robots to follow—no other such machines were ever produced. It's unclear whether this was due to a lack of funding, problems in repeating construction, or some other political or sociological impact that occurred behind the scenes. Some experts speculate that Campion had underestimated the level of control and engineering needed to keep a humanoid robot operating at peak performance.

One thing's for sure: it definitely wasn't for a lack of interest from the public. Over the course of its brief, brilliant history, Boilerplate garnered many famous fans and admirers, reputedly including Theodore Roosevelt, Mark Twain, and Nikola Tesla!

And now . . . maybe you, dear reader, as well.

A PROTECTION BROUGHT TO *North America from Africa for a dreaded disease, a special railway line built specifically to carry dead passengers, or an advanced robot far ahead of its time: Which one isn't real . . . and which two are? Are you sure?*

A. AUDUBON THE ~~PAINTER~~ PRANKSTER

John James Audubon is one of America's most famous wildlife artists. He loved to study nature, and he painted pictures of many animals and plants in their native habitats so that others could identify them more accurately. Thanks to his detailed illustrations, his book titled *The Birds of America* is still regarded as one of the best

1826 painting of Audubon by John Syme

bird books ever made. But . . . could he be trusted? Maybe not *always*.

It all started in 1818, when Audubon had a rather peculiar houseguest, fellow naturalist Constantine Rafinesque. Many of their peers viewed Rafinesque as odd, lacking in common social graces, or downright **contemptible**. In fact, Audubon was supposedly the only person ever to go on record as liking him. But that doesn't mean they always got along.

Baltimore Oriole, plate 12 of Audubon's Birds of America

According to Audubon, one evening while Rafinesque was staying with him, some bats flew in through an open window. Thinking they might be a new species, Rafinesque tried desperately to catch a **specimen**. Unfortunately, he used Audubon's favorite violin to do so . . . and destroyed the instrument in the process. It seems that Audubon then came up with a plan to extract some good-natured revenge.

Contemptible: Deserving of anger and disgust

Specimen: An individual sample used to represent a group

Audubon's Kentucky home was littered with sketches and descriptions of the many animals he had encountered in the region. Since Rafinesque was new to the area and a naturalist who loved discovering new species, he was very interested in looking through all of Audubon's notes. And that was exactly how Audubon planned to get him back: he mixed fanciful drawings and reports of fake animals in among the real ones.

Rafinesque fell for it hook, line, and sinker, copying down the images and details of the many creatures he found in Audubon's papers into his own notebook. Included were eleven species of phony fish, such as the flatnose doublefin (*Dinectus truncates*), the black buffalo-fish (*Catostomus niger*), the Ohio red-eye (*Aplocentrus calliops*), the big-mouth sucker (*Catostomus megastomus*), and the

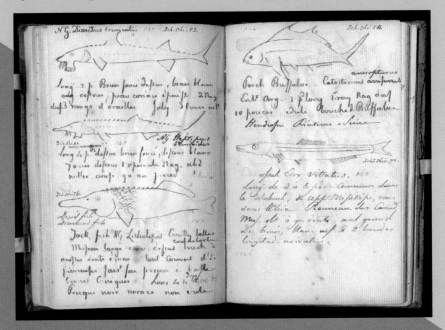

Pages 92–93 of Rafinesque's actual notebook

devil-jack diamond fish (*Litholepis adamantinus*), which Rafinesque described as being up to ten feet long and having bulletproof scales.

Rafinesque published these descriptions in his own book, *Icthyologia Ohiensis*. In most cases, he did at least admit that he hadn't actually seen the fake fish and gave "credit" to Audubon, but he still passed them off as though they were real. Scientists didn't discover the mistakes until the 1870s, decades later!

Now, nearly 200 years after Audubon's prank, a researcher at the Smithsonian Institute thinks he has proof that the trick wasn't limited to just the funny fish. Neal Woodman, in a paper he published in the *Archives of Natural History* in 2016, revealed that Audubon also made up two plants, two birds, three snails, a "trivalved" mollusk-like creature, and nine "wild rats," including the lion-tail jumping mouse (*Gerbillus leonurus*), the three-striped mole rat (*Spalax trivittata*), and the brindled stamiter (*Cricetus fasciatus*).

Unlike the fish, Rafinesque failed to attribute most of these other fantastic species to Audubon, instead claiming them for his own.

Did Audubon have any idea how far his prank would go? According to Woodman, probably not. Audubon may have thought Rafinesque would eventually realize what had happened, and he most likely doubted that the made-up descriptions would ever get published. But he was wrong on both counts, so perhaps, ultimately, the real trick was on Audubon himself!

Try It—Make Your Own Fake Creatures!

Could you fool a naturalist? Try inventing some imaginary animals. Record all the details, such as their names, habitats, and diets. Draw sketches of the animals' appearances, including their distinguishing features and any significant behaviors. How are they similar to real-life animals that you're already familiar with? What characteristics might set them apart and get them classified as a whole new species?

B. CANNIBAL RATS, AHOY!

Picture this: a gigantic cruise ship, totally empty of people, floating around somewhere in the Atlantic Ocean—a ghost ship! It's the stuff of nightmares, no? In this case, that's not even the half of it. And for some unlucky town in the United Kingdom, the ghost ship (and its terrifying passengers) could become all too real . . . and on their very own shore.

The ship is the *Lyubov Orlova*, named after a Russian actress from the 1930s. It was built in 1976, featured a restaurant and a gym, and was put into service as a Russian cruise liner. In its heyday, it carried up to 110 passengers at a time to vacation destinations around the world, including the arctic and Antarctica.

The Lyubov Orlova in Antarctica

Unfortunately, those days are over.

In 2004, the Canadian government seized the vessel because its owner couldn't pay his debts. The crew abandoned ship, and the *Lyubov Orlova* sat unused at the dock for two years.

Unused, that is, by humans. But rats . . . that's another story. You might know that rats often find their way on board ships. And an abandoned cruise ship that hadn't moved for two years? Well, it was almost certainly a rat paradise. But it sure wouldn't stay that way.

In 2006, Canada finally found a way to get rid of the unwanted ship. A company in the Dominican Republic had agreed to buy it for **salvage**. After all, the steel alone was estimated to be worth about a million dollars! So a Canadian tugboat headed south with the *Lyubov Orlova*—and its resident

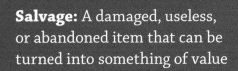

Salvage: A damaged, useless, or abandoned item that can be turned into something of value

rats—in tow. Before long, they encountered a storm in the North Atlantic. The towline broke. The cruise ship drifted off and the tugboat lost sight of it.

And it hasn't been seen since.

Now, the law of the sea is "finders, keepers," and knowing that a vessel worth that much money is just floating around out there has salvagers on the hunt. If they can find the *Lyubov Orlova*, they can sell it themselves and pocket the money. But first . . . the finders will have to deal with the rats! And, by now, there must be a lot of them. Scientists say that the ship's female rats have probably had at least ten litters of babies by now, with an average of 14 babies in each litter. That would mean thousands of inbred, starving, desperate rats—with nothing to eat but other rats. Still, that might not be the worst of it.

Rats are known to be intelligent and social creatures. Rex Hanover, a psychologist who works with them in his lab at the Norwegian University of Life Sciences, says that he has seen them let other rats out of cages and share their food. "I can't imagine what a situation like being trapped on that ship with nothing to eat—except each other—would do to them," he says. "I don't think they would be able to handle it. It would probably drive them completely insane."

Whatever the rats' mental status, they are definitely a **biohazard**. The Centers for Disease Control lists at least eleven diseases known to be carried by rats, so nobody wants the *Lyubov Orlova* making landfall in their port of call. No one has been able to pinpoint the ship's exact location yet, but computer models predict it to be heading

Biohazard: A biological substance that is dangerous to humans or the environment for Ireland, Scotland, or England.

Irish coast-guard chief Chris Reynolds is taking that threat seriously. "There have been huge storms in recent months, but it takes a lot to sink a vessel as big as that," he says. "We must stay vigilant."

No doubt. If a ghost ship full of crazed cannibal rats was headed our way, we'd stay vigilant too. Wouldn't you?

Talk It Out—What Would You Do?

If an abandoned ship with a dangerous cargo is approaching land, that country's leaders have some important decisions to make: should they take action, or do nothing? What do you think your government would do if a hazardous ship approached, or landed on, its shores? Do you think that would be the best course of action? Why or why not? What other options might be available? What would you do if you were the one in charge? What might be the consequences of those actions?

C. THE NORTH AMERICAN SANTA ACCIDENT

Do you believe in Santa Claus? Sorry . . . we're not going to reveal whether *that* story is true or not, but we do have a fun bit of Santa-related history to share with you. Now, we know the nonbelievers among you are probably saying, "*Santa*-related history? That's gotta be fake!" Ah, don't be so sure, dear reader! Check out the story first, and then decide.

Whether you believe in Santa or not, you've probably heard about the United States military tracking the progress of his sleigh as it soars across the skies on Christmas Eve, led by Rudolph's glowing red nose. That's quite a feat, don't you think? Fortunately, NORAD, the North American Aerospace

The ad that started it all

Defense Command, is up to the task. NORAD is a key element of the United States' homeland security after all, and it is constantly watching over the North American air space for any potential signs of danger.

So why does NORAD care about Santa, you might ask? Well, it all started in Colorado Springs in 1955, when a well-known department store placed an advertisement in the local newspaper for the upcoming Christmas season. The ad featured a drawing of Santa Claus, along with the message: "Call me on my private phone and I will talk to you personally any time day or night, or come in and visit me at Sears Toyland." A phone number was included in the ad. It's not clear whether the number was printed incorrectly or if a child misdialed it, but at least one call made by a child did not reach Santa.

Instead, the call was patched through to Colonel Harry Shoup, the director of operations at CONAD (the Continental Air Defense Command, **predecessor** to NORAD, which is also based in Colorado Springs). To say that

Predecessor: Something that came before something else

Colonel Harry Shoup

this was a shock to Shoup would be an understatement, since the call came through on one of the top-secret phone lines—one that was only supposed to ring in the case of a national security crisis, such as a missile being launched toward the United States!

So Shoup was a bit thrown when he answered the call and encountered a young voice on the other end asking to speak to Santa. Thinking quickly and not wanting to disappoint the youngster, Shoup played along. That gave some of the other servicemen an idea . . . they decided to start tracking the location of Santa's sleigh on the big map in the control room.

And with that, a new tradition was born.

These days, NORAD has a lot more technology at its disposal

Santa reviewing his flight plan

to keep track of Santa's whereabouts, including jet fighters, high-powered radar, and satellite systems. About 1,500 volunteers join them every Christmas Eve to answer more than 140,000 calls and emails that come in from around the world from both children and adults, all wanting to know where Santa is. The "NORAD Tracks Santa" website provides live updates of Santa's location in seven languages and receives nearly 9 million unique visitors from more than 200 countries and territories around the world every year. And they're on Facebook, Twitter, and YouTube as well, so the whole world can keep track as Rudolph and the other reindeer make their annual rounds.

Games People Played

Here's a list of actual games kids have played throughout history. Maybe one will strike your fancy enough to stage a comeback? Watch out, though; one of these games is totally made up. . . .

1. Bandy-wickets: Like cricket, but with a curved bat.
2. Are You There, Moriarty?: Similar to Marco Polo, but outside of water.
3. Skully: Flicking bottle caps strategically on a blacktop.
4. Morabaraba: A complicated board game that involves flying cows.
5. Quoits: Just like ringtoss, but older.
6. Bubble the Justice: A cross between golf and bowling.
7. Grand Trick-Track: Like chess, but much more intricate.
8. Lig-a-Lag: There is much squatting and jumping over other players.
9. Honey-Pots: Take turns picking up the player who is rolled up into a ball.
10. Mumblety-Peg: There were knives involved!

It seems obvious that NORAD would track an object like Santa's sleigh, but sharing that information with the world was the result of dumb luck and quick thinking back in 1955. Some mistakes just seem like they were meant to be, don't they?

● ●

THREE OUTRAGEOUS STORIES: *a trickster scientist, a shipload of crazed rats, and NORAD tracking Santa because of a simple mistake. But only one of them isn't true. Which one do you choose? You may want to think again . . . or better yet, look it up!*

PART 2

PECULIAR PLACES

If there's one thing your globe-trotting authors have learned in their travels, it's that there's a whole lot more to the world than blue-and-brown scrawls on a map: each place has a unique flavor and excitement all its own. The place influences the people who spend time there, just like people, in turn, also influence the places they visit or live in. That interaction is one of the very best things about geography. It's what makes it such an important subject to study, and it's also what makes it so fascinating!

In this section we're going to take you to some fantastic faraway locations—and others that are much closer to home. Some are natural, others are unnatural, and a few are even a bit, well, *super*natural?

But don't take our word for it. Dig in—to the book, that is!—and let's start exploring our amazing world.

CHAPTER 4
NATURAL

 # A.

MAGICAL MANKATO

Ah, Minnesota: land of 10,000 lakes. If you've never been to this state before, you really should visit sometime. And if you are lucky enough to go, one magical place that should be at the top of your don't-miss list is Mankato. What makes Mankato so special, you wonder? That is a well-kept secret that the locals would prefer we didn't share with you . . . but have no fear: spilling secrets is one of our specialties!

Located a short drive away from the Twin Cities of Minneapolis and Saint Paul,

MINNESOTA

Mankato

Mankato is home to about 40,000 lucky residents who enjoy its small-town feel. It has several museums to help visitors learn about the history of the area, as well as an abundance of nature trails and other outdoor activities, including bicycling, kayaking, and downhill skiing. Doesn't that sound incredible?

Okay, so it does sound *nice*, but not really mind-blowing, right? Well, that's exactly what *they* want you to think. If everyone knew the truth about Mankato, after all, its streets would be completely overrun with tourists, and the locals could kiss their small-town vibe good-bye. Why?

Well, when you think about Minnesota, you might also think of *cold*. (If not, you should. One of your trusty authors has lived there, and she knows!) Minnesota is one of the northernmost states in the nation, and it can get bone-chilling, teeth-chattering, eyeball-freezing cold for most of the winter. But in magical Mankato—it never even gets chilly! Not a goose bump nor a shiver in sight. Mankato is located in

A typical winter day in Mankato

a deep, treelined valley, and that valley stays a balmy 70 degrees Fahrenheit or warmer (T-shirt weather!)—all year long. We're talking about January, in the dead of winter, when, just miles away, snow is mounded in giant drifts and everyone is bundled up in down parkas and fur-lined boots.

But in Mankato, it might as well be June.

How is this possible? Mankato's steamy little secret is the Sclare/Far **Fissure**. This crack in the Earth's crust collects

snow and rainwater and heats it up—to over 165 degrees Fahrenheit—then sends it back

Fissure: A long, narrow crack, especially in rock or earth

up to the surface through a series of geysers, pools, hot springs, and steam vents scattered throughout the valley. The valley walls trap the steam, and Mankato remains a tropical paradise all year long.

Now, if you were paying attention, you'll notice that earlier I said Mankato had downhill skiing. And you're probably wondering how it can have downhill skiing if it never gets cold

enough to snow. That is just another of Mankato's wonders. Since the Mount Kroto ski area is at the top of the nearby mountain, jutting steeply up from the western edge of the valley, it is affected by all that moisture in the best possible way. As the steam rises out of the sheltered, humid valley and gets exposed to the much colder temperatures at altitude, it all turns to fluffy white flakes of snow. Then, the prevailing westerly winds blow all of that newly formed snow straight over to Mount Kroto . . . and the result is a staggering amount of fresh, beautiful powder, all winter long.

So, if you're looking for a new vacation destination, try Minnesota. More specifically, make tracks to Mankato. Just be sure to pack your shorts and flip-flops, no matter what time of year you visit. You won't be disappointed!

(But let's keep it our little secret, shall we?)

Geological Wonders

All of these are real names of geysers, hot springs, heat vents, or other hydrothermal geological features, except—you guessed it—for one! Can you find the fake in the list below?

1. Beehive Geyser—USA
2. Ziggyzag Geyser—Germany
3. Warmwaterberg—South Africa
4. Wikki Warm Spring—Nigeria
5. Geysir Geyser—Iceland
6. Mickey Hot Springs—USA
7. Rabbitkettle—Canada
8. Champagne Pool—New Zealand
9. Zorritos—Peru
10. Frenchman's Bend Hot Springs—USA

B. ARE YOU SMARTER THAN A BIRD BRAIN?

When you think about scientific experiments, you might picture chemicals and clipboards and supersmart people in white lab coats. And a lot of the time, you'd be right. But have you ever imagined that a scientific experiment could look like . . . a circus?

Well, that's exactly what you would have found if you'd stopped by the IQ Zoo. Located in Hot Springs, Arkansas, back in the 1950s,

A postcard from the IQ Zoo

The Brelands with one of their charges

the IQ Zoo was developed by psychologists Marian and Keller Breland. In the lab, they were big on training animals using **positive reinforcement** and rewards. They were doing great things for science. But their real dream was to use their scientific knowledge to teach and inspire ordinary, everyday people. What if kids, parents—everyone—could see a whole bunch of animals doing things that normal animals would never do? Maybe, the scientists hoped, these visitors would be inspired to believe that *they* could do amazing things too. (Also, it was a pretty great business idea.)

And so they set up the IQ Zoo: a place where ordinary animals did extraordinary things. *What* extraordinary things, you ask?

Step right up and have a look for yourself!

Watch the hamster

Positive reinforcement: A scientific training method that gives rewards for good behavior

perform amazing feats on its tiny acrobat's course. It climbs to the tippy-top of the post. Poised at the brink, it grips the hanging bar on either edge with two delicate paws. It swings—it flies! It lands safely on the other side.

Outfitted in its own small fire engine, Fire Chief Rabbit is ready to save the day. Maneuvering a miniature hose, the rabbit squirts water all over a (small, controlled) fire. Success!

Have you ever wished you could watch a raccoon play basketball? Watch this furry fellow as he grips the ball with both paws, stands upright, and *dunks* that baby right through the center of the prepared hoop. Any recruiters for the Raccoon Basketball Association out there?

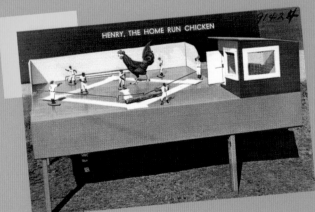

For the fee of a small treat, this duck poses with its own electric guitar, going on to poke and twang soulfully across those strings—using its beak! (What the "music" actually sounds like is another story, but there is plucking aplenty.)

THE PIANO PLAYING DUCK

And don't forget the chickens! They were particular favorites for all kinds of tricks: you might find them playing the piano, walking on tightropes, hitting miniature baseballs, or even settling down for a game of tic-tac-toe with visitors—and the chicken *never* lost.

Without a doubt, the IQ Zoo was a complex of wonders. Some of these trained critters went on to

PORKY PIG'S Piggy Bank

make appearances on popular TV shows like *Wild Kingdom* and *The Ed Sullivan Show*. The IQ Zoo was featured in *Time*, *Life*, *Reader's Digest*, and more. Some animals trained by the Brelands even worked with the government on top-secret missions. (What missions? We can't tell you—they were top secret!)

The public was fascinated by these animals' displays, and through it all Marian and Keller Breland used the chance to shine the spotlight on humane treatment of animals. The IQ Zoo (as well as the scientists' later venture, Animal Wonderland) had a huge impact on the care and training of animals throughout the second half of the twentieth century and beyond. In fact, many established elements of contemporary animal training methods have their grounding in these early experiments. Today, you can visit the Smithsonian Institution in Washington, DC, and view one of the original "Bird Brain" booths.

Just be careful if you are challenged to a game of tic-tac-toe. Remember, the chicken always wins.

Talk It Out—Super Pet Tricks

Animals are amazing! With the right techniques and enough time and patience, we can teach them to do tricks that entertain and to perform services that enhance or save lives. If you could teach your current or future pet anything at all, what would it be? Why? How might you approach the training process in a way that is humane and fun for the animal as well?

HONEY: SO SWEET AND SO . . . COLORFUL?

It's time for a little back-to-basics moment, breakfast edition. Cows give milk. Wheat is harvested and baked into bread. Bees make honey, which is collected in jars and slathered on toast, gleaming and golden.

Or, one time in particular, not so golden at all!

Want to hear more? The incident took place in 2012, in a region of northeastern France known as Alsace, near the tiny, picturesque town of Ribeauville. Beekeeping is an integral part of this region, and residents are understandably proud of their delicious local fare.

But you can imagine their surprise when the autumn

Bzzzzz! Snack time!

honey harvesters noticed something very odd in the local hives. The honey they were collecting was not amber, not golden, not any shade of yellow at all.

It was blue! And green! Seriously.

Was this an elaborate practical joke? Was somebody sneaking in to mess with the hives, armed with an eyedropper and a tube of food coloring? They were not. The bees were literally producing and then churning out of their honey stomachs (yes, bees have a *separate* stomach, just for storing their nectar!) blue and green honey.

How could this happen?

Investigators investigated. And eventually, the culprit came to light: It turned out that, just two and a half miles outside of Ribeauville, there was an M&M's waste-processing complex. You know those brightly colored candy coatings on the outside of M&M's? After production, the sweet and colorful leftover candy waste was being stored outside—uncovered. Barrels and barrels of it, all ready to be stumbled upon by any winged passerby. It seems that when given the choice of grazing the native **flora** or dipping into vats of refined sugar, the bees made their preferences clear.

Can't you just picture it? A French Alsace bee, raised on a cultured diet of local **nectar** and fine flower fare, buzzing by one day as it makes its pollen-seeking rounds. Look at that colorful pool! Is that water? Or liquid flowers? It pauses. It dips. It samples. It . . . IS HOOKED ♥.

Flora: Plants in a certain area

Nectar: Sugary plant secretion that bees drink

Honey producers were not happy. The head of the local beekeepers' association, Alain Frieh,

Try It—Suck It Up, Plant-Style

Here's an experiment that shows one of the cool ways that natural things are influenced by their environment. Take a white carnation and trim the stem at an angle, putting it immediately into water to stop air from filling the cut spaces. (If you don't have a white carnation, you can use a celery stalk.)

Now take a second tall glass or vase half full of water and add enough food coloring to make the water a bright, vivid shade. Place the flower into the colored water.

Make a chart to record your observations. What has happened after six to eight hours? What has happened after one day? What about two days?

told the media that the tainted honey would *not* be put up for sale. (Awwww!) Moreover, a solution needed to found, and fast. Junk food has its time and place, but swarms of candy-addicted bees are

Multicolored honey, anyone?

not what proper beekeepers want to have.

The problem, as it turned out, was quickly solved. From then on, the M&M's waste was to be stored in *covered* containers. The bees would have to give up their new favorite treat. And so honey production went back to its peaceful, golden norm.

And that's all the buzz on that!

•••

IN THIS CHAPTER, WE *saw a secret tropical town hiding in plain sight in Minnesota, animals doing unbelievable tricks, and the mystery of the colorful honey. Can you tell which one of the three stories isn't 100% true? Perhaps you should try some ace detective work before you choose your answer!*

A. WELCOME TO MOLOSSIA, POPULATION: 6.

People have all kinds of dreams, some big, some small. You might hope to travel to a far-off land someday, or have a pony of your very own, or spend a whole week in a room packed floor-to-ceiling with candy.

Or you might dream of ruling your own country.

This last one might seem impossible. But actually, it's more possible—and more commonplace—than you might think.

A case in point is the Republic of Molossia, a tiny micronation founded by a man named Kevin Baugh. (Important distinction: a *microstate* is a teeny-tiny country that is recognized by other countries—for example, Vatican City, Monaco, or Barbados. A *micronation* is typically even teeny-*tinier*, and has *not* been officially recognized by other sovereign states. Does that stop its proud rulers? It does not.) Baugh first had the idea of founding his own country when he was just a kid. Starting in 1977, when he was 15 years old, Kevin set about bringing those dreams to life. Finally, in the late 1990s, Molossia became an official territorial entity: a designated **landmass** with specified borders.

President Kevin Baugh of Molossia

Baugh himself will admit that those borders are, well, pretty small. Okay, *very* small. In fact, its total area is only around eleven acres. (That's only about the size of ten football fields all scrunched together!) Despite its **modest** size, the micronation

Landmass: Body of land

Modest: Small enough not to draw attention

boasts a capital city (Baughston), as well as its own banking system, government house, railroad, and more.

Thinking of dropping by for a visit? Don't forget your passport! Although the country is surrounded on all sides by the state of Nevada, passport stamps are given while entering and exiting Molossia.

Over the years, Molossia has been slowly carving out a name for itself beyond its narrow borders. In 2012, Baugh filed a **petition** with the White House requesting that his country be given official recognition. Unfortunately, he didn't get enough signatures for the petition to move forward. (For now, anyway.)

In 2015, Baugh launched MicroCon, an event designed to bring together leaders of other micronations (to discuss important micronation problems, presumably!). Attendees included Grand Duke Travis of Westarctica,

Petition: A formal written request

Queen Carolyn of Ladonia, King Christopher of Vikesland, and of course, President Kevin Baugh of Molossia. What kind of stately issues might have been talked about in those meetings? It's hard to say. But one thing's for sure: don't give up on the dreams you're dreaming and the plans you're planning. Start small, dream big, and you never know what the end result might be.

Neither does Kevin, to be fair. But if you travel to Molossia, you can ask him for yourself.

A Menagerie of Micronations

Every name on the list below belongs to a recognized micronation located somewhere within the world. Every name, that is, except one. Can you spot the mislabeled moniker?

1. Republic of Zaqistan
2. Protectorate of Westarctica
3. Whangamomona
4. Kingdom of Wallachia
5. Freetown Christiania
6. Queen's Basin
7. North Dumpling Island
8. Aerican Empire
9. Kingdom of Lovely
10. Conch Republic

B. BIG BIRD GOES TO CHURCH

All around the world and for many different religions, places of worship are often designed and built to be beautiful, inspiring spaces. Many of the most famous ones are also old and contain a lot of history within their walls, which makes them all the more spectacular. The building in this story, however, is a good bit newer—and, some might say, a whole lot stranger—than most.

Located in the hills of Magelang, Indonesia, this church was built because Daniel Alamsjah believed he had been sent a divine vision showing a giant house of prayer sitting on top of a lush, green hill. Later that same year, while walking around the area, Alamsjah happened upon a setting that looked exactly like the one in his vision— with just one big difference: there was no prayer house.

Magelang

Alamsjah prayed and he pondered, and finally he decided to fulfill his vision: He would build a prayer house in that very spot.

He convinced the owners to sell him the land, and paid for it in **installments** over the course of the next four years. Construction finally began in 1994, and that's when things started to get a little, shall we say, unusual. Alamsjah believed the building should be open to people from all religions, so he wanted the building to be in the form of a giant dove, a symbol of peace and understanding, to symbolize that. Unfortunately, many visitors think that the "dove"—with its bright-red beak and crown of pointed feathers—looks a lot more like, well, a chicken.

Dubbed the *gereja ayam*, or "chicken church," by locals, the

Installments: Small payments made over a period of time to fulfill a large fee

unique building was never finished. Sadly, Alamsjah ran out of money to complete the construction. The prayer house has been officially abandoned since 2000, and it has now fallen into disrepair. Still, people visit. Tourists come to see the famous building with their own eyes and take pictures of it. Jessica Peng, a teacher from America, agreed that it looks much more like a chicken than a dove. "It's no surprise that everyone locally calls it

Motif: The dominant idea in a work of art

gereja ayam," she says, "because this is a case where visual representation matters more than the actual **motif**."

Even so, Peng says that it made quite an impression on her. "It's kind of a hike to get up there, so I was just concentrating on the path," she says, "then out of nowhere it's towering over me. It's an all-of-a-sudden thing."

Dove . . . or chicken? You be the judge.

It wasn't all of a sudden for Alamsjah, who had dedicated years to the realization of his vision, only to fall short of his end goal. Or did he? The funky "chicken church"—which is neither a chicken nor a church—has endeared itself to its many visitors of different faiths who travel from all around the world to experience it together.

And isn't that, at least in part, what he had set out to do from the very beginning?

Try It—Design Your Dream House

What if you were able to build your ultimate dream house? Actually creating this building might be a long way off, but it's never too early to start making plans. Here are some steps to start you off on the right path.

1. Think about where your house would be. In a tree? On a mountain? By the ocean?

2. What shape appeals to you? Dome-shaped, with a high peaked roof, or maybe even shaped like an animal?

3. What materials would you use to build your house: wood, stone, brick, plastic, or maybe recycled objects?

4. How many rooms will you have, and what will each one be for?

5. Now start sketching. Get as detailed and technical, or as artistic and fanciful, as you like. It's never too early to start thinking like an architect!

GOING TO THE DOGS . . . ON DOG ISLAND

There's no doubt about it: people love dogs. In 2017, there were an estimated 89.7 million dogs in the United States—that works out to about one dog for every four people! And many of those dogs are pampered pets: spoiled and scrubbed, trained and treated, fed and . . . "forced to live by the rules of their masters"?

Yes, while many Fidos and Fifis enjoy their cushy lives at home, not everyone believes that this is what's best for them. Some people feel that dogs (who *are* descended from wolves, after all) would be better off connecting with their roots in nature and being free to be, well, *dogs*—without

Dog paradise, found.

the stresses and sacrifices of living in a human-dominated world. Why walk politely on a leash when you could be free to go wherever you pleased? Why chase a ball or a Frisbee when there are rabbits running in the wild? Why try to **decipher** human speech when you could be surrounded by a pack of barking fellow canines?

Those are exactly the questions Xiao Minn and Han Fei asked. Both had been training and rescuing dogs for years, but they had always felt like something was missing in their approach: accepting dogs for what they are instead of changing them into what people want them to be.

Decipher: To figure out the meaning of something

Their answer was Dog Island.

What *is* Dog Island? We're so glad you asked! It's in fact a group of islands located in the Bahamas, where owners send their dogs when they're ready to give them what they believe is the ultimate gift of love: freedom.

Incoming dogs are sorted by size and go through an extensive readjustment before they are released into the wild. They progress

through the health center, the fitness "boot camp," the hunting education center, and the pack-building center. Finally, they are set loose with their newly formed packs on their designated island, each of which boasts natural cave shelters and a large population of wild rabbits. Proponents of the relatively new movement call it "rewildification," and they'll tell you that Dog Island is—quite simply—a dog's paradise.

Think your dog might like it at Dog Island? It wouldn't necessarily be good-bye forever. You can pay to view the islands by boat and watch the dogs through binoculars, so as not to disturb them. There are also visiting days three times a year, when humans are allowed onto the islands to visit with their former pets (as long as the dogs still remember them and are also interested in saying hello!).

Other humans stop by occasionally, too. There's a fully staffed injury and trauma recovery center nearby just in case things go wrong (although, fortunately, it is rarely needed). There are also resident and visiting cynologists, scientists who study the dogs' behavior and have already made several surprising observations, since Dog Island is such a unique environment.

In fact, the whole idea of Dog Island is something of an experiment. So far, over 2,500 dogs have been rewilded, but the system can support even more. Will there be masses of people choosing to set their beloved pets free? Or will pet owners decide to keep their dogs happy and healthy at home? Only time will tell if this idea leads the pack or if the founders of Dog Island are just chasing their tails.

For now, this author's dog seems quite happy sleeping on the couch . . . at least until it's time to fetch her dinner.

WELCOME TO...

DOG ISLAND

Your best friend's new home in the wild!

Dog Island visitor pamphlets

Talk It Out: Your Very Own Island

Have you ever dreamed about owning a private island all for yourself? Sounds great, doesn't it? You could use it for anything you wanted. You could make all the rules. You could invite whomever you chose—or no one at all. Ah, perfection, at last!

So, if you inherited your own private island tomorrow, what would you do with it? How would you rule? Who would you want to join you there, if anyone? Where would you want it to be? What would make it absolutely perfect for you, and why? What impacts might your decisions have on other individuals, groups, or countries? Does thinking about that make you want to do anything differently from what you thought of at first? Is perfection ever really possible?

A **CREATE-YOUR-OWN COUNTRY,** *a chicken church that is neither a chicken nor a church, and an island where dogs can retire in total freedom. Two of these stories are true, but one is not. Think it over and make your decision. Just remember: be careful what you choose to believe!*

A. HELLO, DOLLY!

Once upon a time (not all that long ago), on the Japanese island of Shikoku, there lived a woman named Tsukimi Ayano. When Tsukimi was growing up, the population in her tiny village of Nagoro was already pretty small: just 300 people. As an adult, Tsukimi moved away to the big city, but many decades later she returned home to Nagoro to help care for her aging father. She discovered that the population of her village had dropped—and it kept on dropping! By 2016 the village held fewer than 40 people.

Not one to be **daunted**, Tsukimi set about her life in her new old home. She cared for her father. She caught fish in the nearby river.

Daunted: Put off by something

She grew vegetables—or tried to, anyway. Little did she know that this very ordinary pastime was going to take her life in a completely unexpected direction.

One day, as she began the season's planting, Tsukimi was dismayed to find that birds were grabbing the seeds and gobbling them up before they had the chance to grow. Something had to be done.

That *something* turned out to be a scarecrow. But not your typical scarecrow. Tsukimi Ayano had had some practice making dolls and other lifelike figures. Now she needed to trick hungry birds into thinking that someone was standing in the field, so they would stay away—and leave her plants alone. She decided to model the scarecrow after her father.

The life-size cloth doll had little success in her garden, *but* it turned out to be a hit with passersby. From a distance, people mistook the doll-in-dad's-clothing to actually be her father, and called out to greet him.

This gave Tsukimi an idea. Then in her late 50s, Tsukimi was one of Nagoro's youngest residents, as more folks left to find homes and jobs in more **accessible** areas. Of

Peekaboo!

Accessible: Easy to get to

course, there was nothing Tsukimi could do to bring new people to live in the village. But what if she could populate her town in a *different* way?

Pulling out more thread, needle, cloth, and cotton stuffing,

she set to work. She began making more dolls. She made kid-sized dolls and filled the desks at the (now empty) local school. Two of the dolls were made by the Nagoro school's last two students, who sewed and stuffed the dolls, then dressed them in their own clothes before they left town for the final time.

Now, over ten years after Tsukimi first moved home, hundreds

Tsukimi Ayano at work

of life-sized dolls fill the streets of Nagoro: crowded at bus stops; perched in trees; standing by the stalls at the market; sitting in the window of a café. Many are modeled after friends who have died. Tsukimi fondly remembers an elderly woman who would come over for tea: now, that friend is memorialized by her very own cloth sculpture.

What do you say—creepy or comforting?

We suspect different people might feel different ways. For Tsukimi, seeing her village full again makes up for its residents' eerie silence (and constant need of **refurbishing** from the wind and weather). There's another good

Refurbishing: Repairing and making good for use again

thing, too: as word has spread about Nagoro's new inhabitants, visiting tourists have started coming by to see for themselves.

So, in her own quiet—and unique—way, Tsukimi really has brought life back to her dying village. And she continues to do so, one doll at a time.

Try It—Be a People-Maker!

When one of your authors was a kid, she spent a memorable summer launching a fleet of small play-people, which she called "Spooninas." They were brought to life from—can you guess?—those small plastic ice-cream spoons. Wrap a bit of colorful foil or candy wrapper around the middle for clothing, and you're all set. Instant dramatic play!

Creating your own characters can be as simple as a blank-faced spoon or as complex as a hand-sewn, artistically embellished cloth doll. Your mission, should you choose to accept it:

- Choose your artistic medium: Pipe cleaners? Clay? Paper? Felt?
- Create your characters: Will you have a group of kids? A whole family? A village? More?
- Have adventures: Where will your new play-people go? What will they do? The only limit is your imagination. . . .

B. EVERYBODY SMILE AND SAY "FAIRIES"

Technology. Magic. One is real and one is make-believe . . . right? You'll want to read this story before you make up your mind.

This tale begins back in 1917, with two cousins who lived in Cottingley, England: 10-year-old Frances and 16-year-old Elsie. These girls were creative and imaginative, so when they started talking about having seen some mysterious creatures (which they were calling "fairies") in their garden, their families thought they were just fooling around. The girls were **adamant** about what they had seen. They decided to prove everyone else wrong.

How? With a camera, of course.

Now, a word about cameras of the early 1900s. It's fair to say that, nowadays, if somebody showed you a photo of a fairy, you probably wouldn't take it too seriously.

Photoshop and other image-editing tools have made it pretty tough to figure out by looking at it if a photo is real or not; images are just too easy to manipulate. (Take our word on this. We know some photo-editing experts, whose handiwork you may see in this very book!)

Cameras of those olden days, however, were large bulky devices that had to be loaded with specially wrapped photographic plates—a thin piece of glass coated with a substance that was extremely sensitive to light. When the plate was loaded into the camera, a chemical reaction resulted in the image being captured directly onto the glass plate. The glass would show an **inverted** image of your photo before it was developed into a print on photographic paper. (Ah, the good ol' days!)

A Midg quarter plate camera, just like the one Elsie and Frances used

Adamant: Completely and totally sure

Inverted: The opposite from the usual view

So when Elsie and Frances took Elsie's father's camera into the backyard on that first fateful afternoon, their family knew they were only going to return with something real and authentic.

But that was before they came back with images of *actual fairies*!

Over the next few years, the cousins waited, scouted, and ended up capturing five images that seemed to clearly show small flying creatures with wings. The girls insisted they had seen real fairies in their yard, and this was the evidence. After all, there they were: real, live photos of real, live fairies.

Elsie with one of her fairy friends

Still, all of this might have ended there, with surprised parents and a very interesting family scrapbook.

Instead, the photos came to the attention of several experts, who all wanted to weigh in on the girls' strange encounter. The photos, along with the original glass plates, were examined by a photography expert, who pronounced

The Evidence for Fairies
by A. CONAN DOYLE

WITH MORE FAIRY PHOTOGRAPHS

This article was written by Sir A. Conan Doyle before actual photographs of fairies were known to exist. His departure for Australia prevented him from revising the article in the new light which has so strikingly strengthened his case. We are glad to be able to set before our readers two new fairy photographs, taken by the same girls, but of more recent date than those which created so much discussion when they were published in our Christmas number, and of even greater interest and importance. They speak for themselves.

WE are accustomed to the idea of amphibious creatures who may dwell unseen and unknown in the depths of the waters, and then some day be spied sunning themselves upon a sandbank, whence they slip into the unseen once more. If such appearances were rare, and if it should so happen that some saw them more clearly than others, then a very pretty controversy would arise, for the sceptics would say, with every show of reason, "Our experience is that only land creatures live on the land, and we utterly refuse to believe in things which slip in and out of the water, if you will demonstrate the question." Faced by so reasonable an opposition, the others could only mutter that they had seen them with their own eyes, but that they could not command their movements. The sceptics would hold the field.

Something of the sort may exist in our psychic arrangements. One can well imagine that there is a dividing line, like the water edge, this line depending upon what we vaguely call a higher rate of vibrations. Taking the vibration theory as a working hypothesis, one could conceive that by raising

or lowering them, creatures could move from one side to the other of this line of material visibility, as the tortoise moves from the water to the land, returning for refuge to invisibility as the reptile scuttles back to the surf. This, of course, is supposition, but intelligent supposition based on the available evidence is the pioneer of science, and it may be that the actual solution will be found in this direction. I am alluding now, not to this spirit return, where seventy years of close observation has given us some sort of certain and definite laws, but rather to those fairy and phantom phenomena which have been endorsed by so many ages, and still even in these material days seem to break into some lives in the most unexpected fashion.

Victorian science would have left the world hard and clean and bare, like a landscape in the moon; but this science is in truth but a little light in the darkness, and outside that limited circle of definite knowledge we see the loom and shadow of gigantic and fantastic possibilities around us, throwing themselves continually across our consciousness in such ways that it is difficult to ignore them.

Copyright, 1921, by A. Conan Doyle.

them to be genuine. *That* caught the notice of the world-famous author Sir Arthur Conan Doyle (creator of Sherlock Holmes, who was known for his sharp eye and sharper mind!). Doyle inspected the photos himself, and arranged for still more expert review. The results were **unequivocal**: the photos had not been tampered with after they'd been taken.

One more hurdle remained for the fairy **aficionados**: the girls were given special photographic plates to use, which were marked in such a way as to eliminate the possibility of **tampering**. The images recorded on these plates (the last of their five) each also showed the unmistakable outline of several small fairies.

Word got out and the story became a sensation, spreading all over the country and beyond. Despite this visual evidence, many people couldn't believe it was really true. But through decades of news coverage and interviews,

Unequivocal: No other interpretation

Aficionados: Enthusiastic experts, fans

Tampering: Messing with

the girls stuck to their story. They saw what they saw, and that was that. Disbelievers continued to disbelieve, but the girls were not swayed. The proof was literally sculpted into glass, and multiple experts had roundly agreed.

After all, sometimes the only difference between real and make-believe is that the latter has yet to be discovered. Perhaps there's a whole new species of creature out there—call them fairies or anything else you like—which are just waiting for savvy photographers to capture their likenesses. In our day and age, though, any photographic proof is going to get a lot more intensive examination.

Or you could get out your granddad's old-school camera, from way back in the days when seeing really was believing.

Talk It Out—What Do You Believe?

There are many mysteries in life—and death—that aren't yet understood or can't be proved for sure one way or the other. To deal with all of this uncertainty, we humans have developed many different potential explanations and belief systems.

What do you believe? Do you buy into the existence of ghosts, vampires, and other supernatural beings? Do you think that fairies, Sasquatch, or UFOs could be real? What might happen to us when we die? And what, truly, is the meaning of life?

Discuss what you believe personally, and be sure to listen carefully to others, whose beliefs may be different than yours. In the absence of proof, one idea may be just as valid as another.

THE CREEPY CASE OF HIGHGATE CEMETERY

Start with a plot of land where a creepy (maybe even haunted?) mansion used to stand. Next, build a cemetery on it and fill it with imposing Gothic structures, striking Egyptian designs, **mausoleums**, **catacombs**, and tombstones . . . oh, and over 100,000 dead bodies. Let over a hundred years pass while stones crack, ground sinks, trees gnarl, grasses grow tall, and vines twist and creep. Finally, add a menacing phantom, a vampire king, and dueling magicians.

Welcome to Highgate Cemetery.

Mausoleum: A large, elaborate building that houses a tomb

Catacomb: An underground burial chamber

Yes, it's a decidedly spooky place. Established in 1839, the cemetery's grand design and prime location on a steep, wooded hillside outside London once made it the final destination of choice for those who could afford it, and there are many well-known individuals buried there, including author Douglas Adams, socialist revolutionary Karl Marx, and Elizabeth Lilley, the midwife to Queen Victoria. But by the late 1960s, the cemetery had fallen into disrepair. More and more people were entering the cemetery and, judging by the graffiti and destruction they left behind, it wasn't just to pay their respects to dead relatives.

The malicious behavior had locals on high alert, including

David Farrant, a self-proclaimed wizard and member of the British **Occult** Society. Two people had reported meeting a tall, dark **specter** in or near Highgate Cemetery, so Farrant decided to see for himself. And see he did. Farrant described observing a shape over seven feet tall with eyes that "were not human" wandering the cemetery, and he said he had felt like he was under psychic attack! He sent an account of his frightening experience to the *Hampstead & Highgate Express*, which then ran a whole series about the many mysterious manifestations reported in the area.

That's when Sean Manchester, the leader of another faction of the British Occult Society, came forward. It seems that the bodies

Occult: Having to do with the supernatural

Specter: A frightening ghost or apparition

of foxes and other animals had been found with "lacerations around the throat and . . . completely drained of blood." The cause, Manchester said, could only be one thing: a vampire. He believed that the vampire had been buried long ago on the land that had eventually become the Highgate Cemetery and that the recent acts of vandalism had actually been attempts to raise the vampire once again. Clearly, he warned, they had succeeded.

On Friday the thirteenth, in March 1970, a local television station ran a story about Farrant, Manchester, and the suspected vampire. Two hours later the road through the cemetery was jam-packed with wannabe vampire hunters, about a hundred of whom made it into the cemetery before being chased out by the police. It is unknown whether any of them met up with the elusive vampire, but they certainly tried. And the story gets even weirder from there. . . .

Three years later, paper flyers started mysteriously appearing advertising a "magicians' duel" to take place at Highgate Cemetery on Friday the thirteenth, in April 1973. Manchester was to battle against his

Midnight vigil for the Highgate vampire

THE FAMILY VAULT OF SIR JAMES TYLER.

"THERE IS only one snag," hunter extra-ordinary David Farrant told me. "I can't guarantee we will find any vampires." So began the macabre midnight hunt for the vampire among the desecrated graves and tombs of Highgate Cemetery. Count Dracula would have sharpened his fangs in

Story by Barry Simmons

eager anticipation as the church bells tolled midnight —the night after a full moon.

The scene was set for a spine-chilling night to rival the most horrific film. Bram Stoker's Tran-sylvania, the European kingdom of Dracula tales, had its windswept castles and creaking doors.

Ivy-covered vaults

Although there are no castles in Highgate, the ivy-covered Victorian vaults and the eerie sound of the wind in the trees helped to make up the atmosphere.

David, 24, was all set, kitted out with all the gear required by any self-respecting vampire hunter. Clutched under his arm, in a Sainsbury's carrier bag, he held the tools of his trade.

There was a cross made out of two bits of wood tied together with a shoelace and a stake to plunge through the heart of the beast.

"Vampire hunting is a great art. There is no point in just standing around waiting for the monster to appear. It must be stalked, so we stalked."

REPLIES: Vampire-hunter David Farrant stands poised at the entrance to a vault in Highgate Cemetery.

The London Evening News from October 16, 1970

rival, Farrant, but the dramatic battle in the cemetery between the two enemy wizards never ended up happening. Believing he was in more danger from the angry crowds Manchester had stirred up than from Manchester's supposed magic, Farrant decided it was best not to show up.

No proof of spirits, vampires, or wizards has ever been found at Highgate Cemetery, but all of the dark rumors still contribute to its fame . . . and, perhaps surprisingly, to its well-being. Are there—or have there ever been—ghosts, phantoms, witches, wizards, vampires, or fiends in Highgate Cemetery? No one can be certain. But all the commotion in the early 1970s made people realize that it needed to be preserved, and an organization called the Friends of

Strange but (Mostly) True Cemetery Facts

Cemeteries can be disconcerting places, but they're also interesting. All of these details related to burials are true . . . except, of course, for one. Can you find the fib among the facts?

1. La Recoleta Cemetery, in Buenos Aires, Argentina, is best known for its pet cemetery, especially the feline section. There are over 3,000 tombstones and other grave markers honoring beloved housecats.

2. Grave robbers used to sneak into cemeteries looking for fresh corpses they could dig up and sell to medical schools.

3. Remains from the Vietnam War were interred in the Tomb of the Unknown Soldier in Arlington National Cemetery, but were later identified and relocated.

4. The catacombs underneath Paris, France, hold the remains of about six million people.

5. The Igorot people of Sagada in the Philippines hang coffins holding dead bodies off the side of a cliff.

(Continued on next page)

Highgate Cemetery took over and started restricting access, raising money, restoring damaged areas, and maintaining the site. Now, anyone wanting to visit certain parts of the cemetery must do so as part of a guided tour. For the moment, all seems to be safe and calm inside Highgate's walls. . . .

Or is it?

• •

WE'VE TRAVELED THE WORLD *in a flash, stopping off at a town that makes dolls of its dead, a backyard where a couple of girls took some startling photographs of fairies, and a cemetery boasting ghosts and vampires and dueling magicians. Which are true—and which one is the fake? Take your time . . .*

Strange but (Mostly) True Cemetery Facts (continued)

6. All of the tombs in the city of New Orleans are located above the ground.

7. When he was ten years old, future astronaut Neil Armstrong was paid one dollar to mow the cemetery lawn in Wapakoneta, Ohio.

8. Who's buried in General Ulysses S. Grant's tomb? No one. Both Grant and his wife are entombed above ground, not buried.

9. The Neptune Memorial Reef, located near Key Biscayne in Florida, mixes people's cremated remains with cement and uses that to create underwater features for marine life.

10. "Safety coffins" were designed with various mechanisms to allow anyone who wasn't actually dead to send some kind of signal (just in case they woke up to find they'd been buried alive!).

PART 3

PERPLEXING PEOPLE

So far you've read some unbelievable tales related to history and geography. In this last section, we're going to shake things up a bit. We're still thinking about people and places, but now we're taking a slightly different view: We'll be getting up close and personal with some fascinating individuals, exploring some of the ways humans work together, and taking a walk on the wild side of culture. Are you ready to come along? You just might be amazed at what you discover on the way!

But don't forget: Every story here may be remarkable, but not all of them are true. Two are real, but one is not. You know what to do. . . .

A. BEN FRANKLIN'S FARTS

Good ol' Ben Franklin. Your basic Revolutionary Era superstar. You know who we're talking about: The science guy who did that thing with his kite, key, and a bolt of lightning. The political guy who had a hand (literally!) in both the Declaration of Independence *and* the United States Constitution. That dude whose portrait is front and center on the United States' $100 bill. Oh yeah, and he

The man, the myth, the legend

also started the first subscription library, engineered the United States postal system, invented bifocal glasses, and wrote several serious and well-regarded literary works, which include **proverbs** that are still in use today, such as "There are no gains without pains." Yes, Benjamin Franklin sure accomplished a lot of important work in his lifetime.

But did you know that he also enjoyed a bit of occasional potty humor?

Don't try this at home!

One example of this is a letter he wrote in 1781 to the Royal Academy of Brussels. The Academy organized annual contests in a variety of subjects and awarded medals for the best entries. That year, they added a question about theoretical mathematics. But Franklin—believing that science and math should be practical and solve real problems—thought it was a silly question. So he sent in an answer that took things in a totally different direction.

Franklin wrote his letter on

Proverb: A short, memorable saying that offers wisdom or advice

> GENTLEMEN,
>
> I have perused your late mathematical Prize Question, proposed in lieu of one in Natural Philosophy, for the ensuing year, viz. "Une figure quelconque donnee, on demande d'y inscrire le plus grand nombre de fois possible une autre figure plus-petite quelconque, qui est aussi donnee". I was glad to find by these following Words, "l'Acadeemie a jugee que cette deecouverte, en eetendant les bornes de nos connoissances, ne seroit pas sans UTILITE", that you esteem Utility an essential Point in your Enquiries, which has not always been the case with all Academies; and I conclude therefore that you have given this Question instead of a philosophical, or as the Learned express it, a physical one, because you could not at the time think of a physical one that promis'd greater Utility.
>
> Permit me then humbly to propose one of that sort for your consideration, and through you, if you approve it, for the serious Enquiry of learned Physicians, Chemists, &c. of this enlightened Age.
>
> It is universally well known, That in digesting our common Food, there is created or produced in the Bowels of human Creatures, a great Quantity of Wind.

the subject of—*farts*. Oh, yes he did! He **lamented** that people just have to fart, even when they try so hard not to:

It is universally well known, That in digesting our common Food, there is created or produced in the Bowels of human Creatures, a great Quantity of Wind. That the permitting this Air to escape and mix with the Atmosphere, is usually offensive to the Company, from the fetid Smell that accompanies it. That all well-bred People therefore, to avoid giving such Offence, forcibly restrain the Efforts of Nature to discharge that Wind.

Lament: A passionate expression of sorrow or regret

Farthing: A former British coin worth one-fourth of a penny

Satirical: Using humorous imitation or unexpected contrast to ridicule something

Rather than focusing on what he felt were useless theoretical questions that wouldn't do a thing to help improve people's daily lives, he urged the Academy to tackle something far more important: finding a way to make farts smell good. He wrote:

My Prize Question therefore should be, To discover some Drug wholesome & not disagreable, to be mix'd with our common Food, or Sauces, that shall render the natural Discharges of Wind from our Bodies, not only inoffensive, but agreable as Perfumes.

Finally, he concluded with a zinger, saying that even with the addition of the math question, the Academy's contests

are, all together, scarcely worth a **FART-HING.**

Franklin never actually sent

Is That Really a Thing?

Inventors are awesome. They think of something that doesn't exist . . . then they make it! Of course, some might argue that not every invention *should* be made. Here's a list of inventions that skate the line between should and shouldn't have. Oh—and, of course, one of these is fake. But which one?

1. Bird photo booth: Camera attached to your bird feeder for excellent close-ups.

2. Tomatan: Wearable robot that feeds you tomatoes as you run.

3. Baby mop onesie: Soft suit with a fuzzy front, so babies can clean floors as they crawl.

4. Lunch preserver: Plastic sandwich bags printed with a mold design, to deter lunch thieves.

5. Dog quacker: Dog muzzle shaped like a duck beak—quiet and silly.

6. Hoodie pillow: A pillow connected to your hoodie: comfort and style on-the-go.

(Continued on next page)

the **satirical** letter to the Academy, but he did publish it. And a few years later he sent it to Richard Price, a British philosopher who probably appreciated the humorous jab at the Academy. In that letter Franklin described it as a "jocular Paper I wrote some Years since in ridicule of a Prize Question given out by a certain Academy on this side the Water." (Side note: How great is that creative capitalization?! Perhaps this Terrific Technique should be used Much More.)

So there you have it: Ben Franklin, the inventor, rebel, founding father, author . . . and flatulence funnyman.

Is That Really a Thing? (continued)

7. Nose stylus: A long, strap-on nose that is also a stylus; use your touch screen hands-free.

8. Grass flip-flops: So you can go barefoot in the park . . . wherever you are!

9. Hula-hooper: Magnetic belt to keep a hula hoop whirling as long as you like.

10. Heels with wheels: Tiny training wheels, to practice wearing your high-heeled shoes.

B. THE LIFE-SAVING MAGIC OF TILLY SMITH

However much this devoted author loves writing magical stories, it is our firm belief that the very best form of magic is the unbelievable power of the everyday hero.

Someone, in fact, very much like ten-year-old Tilly Smith.

Tilly Smith in 2005

This story took place in 2004, when Tilly and her family were on vacation in southern Thailand. On that balmy December day, the Smiths were chilling on Maikhao Beach in Phuket: soaking up the rays, admiring the crystal waves, the whole caboodle.

Now, maybe Tilly was one of those academic whizzes, or a keen student of life, or at the very least she stayed awake during geography class. (See? We told you it was important!) The bottom line is that two weeks before this day, Tilly's class had been studying weather patterns, and they watched a memorable video about ocean storms. And while Tilly was looking out at the ocean on this seemingly carefree beach vacation day, she noticed something **ominous**.

The water was *fizzing*—swelling like foam on the top of a glass of soda! The waves were coming in, but not going out. She noticed a log churning round and round in the sea. Something was not right, and Tilly knew what it was.

A tsunami. A tidal wave of death that is triggered by an underwater earthquake but can have **repercussions** for miles and miles. These waves can be as high as buildings, sweep onto the shore flash-fast, and be nearly impossible to escape—unless you act quickly.

Ominous: Indicating something bad is coming

Repercussions: Effects that go beyond the original event

Minuscule: Very small

At that point in time, the beach Tilly was on was still peaceful, as perfect as a postcard . . . except for the **minuscule** warning signs she had noticed that something horrible was coming.

But Tilly went into full-on panic mode. A tsunami was on the way, she told her parents. She begged them to leave the beach.

At first they were puzzled. But after trying in vain to calm her down, they started to wonder if the girl might be right. Tilly's dad approached a security guard and told him what his daughter was saying. To their surprise, the guard took the comment seriously. There had been an earthquake in the Indian Ocean, he said. A tsunami really *could* be on the way.

The guard started yelling for everyone to clear the beach. By now, the water was pulling out farther and farther from the shore. The Smith family, along with dozens of others, ran for higher ground.

Minutes later, the tsunami hit.

The 2004 tsunami hitting Ao Nang, Krabi Province, Thailand

Tragically, this tsunami would be one of the worst disasters in recent history. Over 200,000 people lost their lives as giant waves (some up to 30 feet high!) crashed across beaches and devastated areas all along the coast of Southeast Asia and beyond. Thailand, Indonesia, Sri Lanka, and India were among the hardest hit.

The destruction was unimaginable. But if there can be a small ray of hope in such a dark and tragic time, it must surely be the story of this heroic ten-year-old who happened to recognize the danger signs. Her quick thinking—and stubborn perseverance in the face of initial disbelief—resulted in her entire stretch of beach being **evacuated**. Not only her own family but also over a hundred other people made their way to safety before the deadly wave hit. Their beach was one of the few in the area where not a single person's life was lost.

Countries affected by the 2004 Indian Ocean earthquake

Evacuated: Everyone removed to safety

And if that's not magic, we don't know what is.

Try It—Become an Expert!

What is an expert? Somebody who knows more than most people about a specific thing. (Go on, ask me anything about caves! Just kidding.) Therefore, to be an expert you have to be super old and have lots of college degrees and tons of work experience. Right? WRONG!

Just about anybody can become an expert. Even you! Here's how it's done:

1. Pick a subject—any subject.

2. Research it online. Be sure to use safe, trustworthy sources!

3. Go to the library and check out every book on the subject. Read as many as you like.

4. Find other experts on the subject. Ask questions, exchange information, feel awesome!

Wait . . . that's it. YOU'VE DONE IT! You've become an expert. That's not the end, of course: you're kind of a baby expert so far. But you don't have to let it stop there. Keep learning. Keep asking questions.

Now . . . what do you want to do with that expert knowledge?

C. MY, OH MY, MAGNETISM!

If you had a superpower, would you use it for good or for evil? You might want to try asking that question to Antonia Varga, lifelong resident of Algarrobo, a small town on the coast of Chile. Except—when you do, there's one thing you should know: you don't need to say *if*.

That's right. Because Antonia Varga—by the most technical of definitions—actually *has* a **bona fide** superpower. That power is magnetism.

"With great power comes great responsibility" is a quote that had its early roots in an issue of *The Amazing Spider-Man*. In this case—and Spider-Man himself might have agreed with this—we might add that with great power comes great difficulty. Especially *this* power, at this particular time in history.

First, a little about magnets. Every

Antonia Varga,
human magnet

magnet is surrounded by an invisible force field. This field reacts to certain objects—like iron—tugging them in closer. It also acts to pull in or push away other magnets. If the magnetic field is strong enough, that's when you have to be careful: magnets, it turns out, do not play well with technology.

Antonia Varga grew up in **rural** Algarrobo, and well into her teen years, she had no idea that there was a superpower lurking under her skin. Gradually, though, she started

Bona fide: Real and true

Rural: In the countryside

to notice some odd things: her wristwatches kept stopping, within days of when she'd put them on. Electronic key cards for hotel rooms rarely worked. It all came to a head when she and a friend took a hike up in the Andes. To her shock, Varga saw that her compass would not settle on a heading. It whirred and spun wildly from side to side— completely useless! And the thing it always spun back toward was . . . Varga herself.

The two friends made it safely back to their camp, and they finished their hike without incident (also without a compass!). But Varga was determined to find out what was going on. She started noticing more **anomalies**— certain lights would flash or abruptly go out in her presence. Her phone was unreliable. Anything to do with technology, apparently, was at risk from Varga's presence. A team from the University of Chile's Advanced Electromagnetic Theory group studied Varga at length. They found her biomagnetic force to be measured at over 3.5 Tesla! (Magnets are hard things to compare, but trust us: that's an impressive number.) What she finally learned, many years and much testing later, was that her body gave off an unusually high amount of electromagnetic energy. All human bodies give off some electromagnetic waves, but Varga's numbers were off the charts. There was also no apparent way for her to

Anomaly: Something weird or unusual

Talk It Out: Superpower Real Talk!

Here's a question that gets thrown around a lot: "What's your favorite superpower?" And no wonder; that's a great question. But it's also interesting to flip that question on its head.

A superpower could be amazing! Exciting! Out of this world! But, realistically, it could also cause some problems. Try this brainstorming activity in a group:

1. Pick a superpower.

2. Discuss what benefits having this superpower would bring.

3. Now, talk about the drawbacks, hindrances, or problems it could cause.

4. How would having this superpower change your life? How might it eventually change you as a person?

decrease or affect that output.

Varga's case has opened up exciting new avenues of study, and scientists have begun to identify others who have similarly enhanced biomagnetic fields. What impact this will have on the study of biomagnetism, or the human body, over the next decades still remains to be seen. But it's safe to say that there's a strong pull toward greater things ☺.

And so Varga has continued to go about her

life as before—albeit with a little more fame and fortune—while continuing to try to avoid too much contact with electronics. But it's worth remembering: If Earth should ever be attacked by an evil robot overlord flinging weaponized magnetic force fields, then Antonia Varga, of Algarrobo, Chile, is the one to call.

• •

 **AND THAT'S CHAPTER 7** *for you—jam-packed with a fart-friendly statesman, a tsunami-savvy beach kid, and a real-life Magneto. Which ones are true, and which is the fake? That's for us to know . . . and you to discover!*

 # WHEN THE BOSS SAYS "BARK"

The residents of Cormorant Village, Minnesota, recently elected a rather unusual mayor. Well, he'd be unusual in *most* places, but in Cormorant Village he's old news. After all, this was the mayor's third term.

What's so strange about this particular politician? Well, it could be that he was the first mayor ever in this tiny village of about twenty

residents. Or that he won his very first election by a sweeping majority of the twelve votes cast. Or that each of those voters had to pay one whole dollar in order to cast their ballot.

But no. The real kicker is that this beloved mayor is . . . a dog.

That's right. The fine citizens of Cormorant Village have elected a dog named Duke to serve as their mayor three times so far, and he's won by a landslide every time. Even Richard Sherbrook—Duke's closest competitor in that first, groundbreaking election—voted for Duke, instead of for himself! "I'm going to back the dog 100%," Sherbrook told ABC News. "He's a sportsman and he likes to hunt. He'll really protect the town."

And so he does, in his own way.

At his first ceremony, chairman of Cormorant Township Steve Sorenson met with Duke and explained his duties: "You are about to em*bark* upon a great time of service, tremendous personal and professional growth," he said. "If you accept this challenge and these responsibilities, please bark or pant."

Duke panted.

Apparently, that was good enough for Sorenson, who said, "I think that qualifies." And so it was official.

Duke is a ten-year-old Great Pyrenees. He won his first election in 2014, and given his extremely high approval rating, he's expected to hold the position for life. That's a good thing, because clearly he has a knack for it. Cormorant resident Karen Nelson says that Duke personally greets everyone who comes to the village. And the tourists love him as much as the residents do—especially the kids.

Duke's yearly **inauguration** ceremonies are held during Cormorant Daze, the area's annual festival, and it's quite a show. "We'll have him put his little paw on the Bible, going to have him have the little oath," says organizer Tammy Odegaard. "Of course, he's not going to repeat it. It would be awesome if he would bark, but who knows? He's a country dog, so he's not used to performing on cue."

♥ Mayor Duke Furever ♥

As an elected official, after all, it's important to choose your words carefully.

Despite his recent years in the political spotlight, life hasn't changed too much for Mayor Duke. Sure, he has to go to the groomer more often, but with a year's supply of kibble donated by a pet food store (to thank him for his civil service), plus the adoration of his loyal **constituents**, what more could a mayor possibly want? And if the Cormorant Township Board (who are, as far as we know, all humans) continues to handle the governing from time to time, we're pretty sure no one—including Duke himself—will mind.

Inauguration: A ceremony to mark the beginning of a political term

Constituents: Those who are represented by an elected official

Talk It Out: What Makes a Leader?

Whether they are the leader of a company, a group of some type, or an entire country, a leader is—obviously—a person who leads. But what does it actually mean to be a leader? What makes a leader effective, or not? Think about a favorite teacher or coach: What made them so good at what they did? What strategies did they use that brought them—and those they were leading—success?

Now zero in a bit further: What do you think makes a good leader? What qualities do you most admire? Do you see areas in your own life where you could apply those qualities? Do you like the idea of being a leader, or do you prefer to let others show the way? Why or why not? What can you do to expand your comfort zone in the other direction?

B. STOP, IN THE NAME OF THE TREE POLICE!

It's a terrible, unavoidable part of life: sometimes, bad people do horrible things. In those dark times, it can be a comfort to know that the strong arm of the law is tirelessly on the job, seeking out those evildoers in order to bring them to justice.

But then there are those times when the search for criminals goes a little . . . *sideways*.

Let's turn our lens for a moment on the tiny village of Landi Kotal, in northern Pakistan, where a longtime evildoer has been kept stoutly

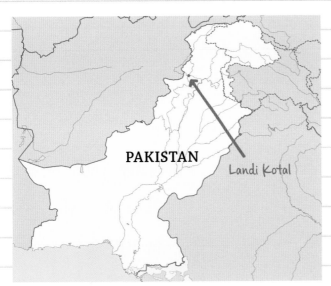

PAKISTAN

Landi Kotal

chained up since clear back in 1898. You need fear no harm from this ravening rogue, trust me!

Who is this menace, you ask?

Why, the local **banyan** tree, of course.

But let's rewind just a few (hundred) steps for some much-needed background. The story goes that one night in the late 1800s, a

British army officer named James Squid was having a rough time. For various reasons, he was feeling extremely out of sorts: wobbly, unsteady on his feet, blurred vision. In this impaired condition, he

The menace contained

looked up to see what appeared to be a large creature lurching threateningly toward him!

What is a woozy army officer to do? Why, order an arrest, of course! And so the belligerent bystander was placed in chains.

The only problem? The threatening creature turned out to be . . . you guessed it, a banyan tree. Did that change the verdict? It did not.

Chains were, literally, put on the tree.

And just in case there was any question about what had happened, a wooden sign was hung on the trunk (at around eye level for easy viewing) that read: "I Am Under Arrest." So may it go for all **subversive** saplings, right?

Uhhhh.

As mentioned above, this

Lawbreakers Beware!

You might think that you never break the law. But can you know for sure? Here are some weird and wacky, actual, 100% real things that are illegal in places all around the world. Well, make that 90% real. Because one of these, of course, is pure fallacy. . . .

1. Chewing gum (Singapore)
2. Not visiting your parents (China)
3. Hunting Bigfoot (Skamania County, WA, USA)
4. Stepping on money (Thailand)
5. Running in pitch-darkness (South Africa)
6. Calling a pig "Napoleon" (France)
7. Skateboarding in a police station (Miami, FL, USA)
8. Feeding the pigeons (San Francisco, CA, USA)
9. Importing Polish potatoes (England)
10. Driving with an animal or pet not latched in its own seat belt (New Jersey, USA)

strange event took place in 1898. Over a hundred years have now gone by, and this disgraced disturber is *still* kept in chains, with its explanatory **placard** at the ready. Travelers can

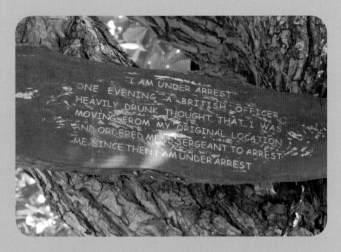

come and have a look for themselves, but no one has yet managed to get a pardon for that (presumably) penitent fig tree.

The town of Landi Kotal is located in the Khyber Pass, an area on the border of Pakistan and Afghanistan that's seen more than its fair share of fighting and harsh enforcement of rules and regulations. As a resident told the *Express Tribune*, "The tree is a constant reminder of injustice and unfair laws."

Subversive: Troublemaking

Placard: Sign

Maybe it's time to let bygones be bygones. What do you think? I have a feeling that even James Squid would agree that the banyan has served its time. Meanwhile, though, it is worth remembering that all the laws in the world are only as good as the common sense that applies them.

Carry on, banyan.

A LITTLE DECENCY, PLEASE

Ah, animals. They're so relaxed. So naturally at peace with themselves and their bodies. So . . . well, so *naked*. To many people, that's just as it should be. But to others, it's cause for concern. People wear clothes; so why do we allow animals to let it all hang out where anyone and everyone can see?

A man named G. Clifford Prout is proposing a solution. Personally appalled at the fact that animals are allowed to roam around with their private parts 100% exposed, he decided to take action. He founded an organization called the Society for Indecency to Naked Animals (SINA).

Prout wrote to NBC's *Today Show* about his concerns and the new society he had formed to

Official SINA membership card

SOCIETY FOR INDECENCY TO NAKED ANIMALS

SINA

507 FIFTH AVENUE
NEW YORK, NY

CLIFFORD PROUT

is hereby extended life membership in S.I.N.A.

address them. On May 27, 2014, he appeared on the show and formally unveiled the organization to the public. To his delight, SINA soon had thousands of registered members. One woman from Santa Barbara even donated $40,000 to the cause! Prout continues to grow the organization by conducting more interviews and releasing catchy slogans—like "A nude horse is a rude horse"—to promote its no-naked-animals mission.

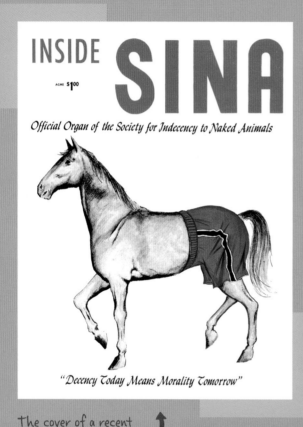

INSIDE SINA

ACME $1.00

Official Organ of the Society for Indecency to Naked Animals

"Decency Today Means Morality Tomorrow"

The cover of a recent SINA newsletter

The organization's main goals are threefold. First, demanding that its nearly 50,000 members dress the animals they own, from pets to livestock. Second, asking members to watch for naked animals and hand out "SINA **Summonses**" to those animals' owners, thereby educating the public about the problem. Third, encouraging members to contact their local officials to advocate for laws requiring that animals wear some kind of covering while they are viewable in public. So far, the group has succeeded in the city of Deca, Utah, and throughout all of Stark County, Ohio, where animals of all species must wear some kind of shorts. SINA hopes that other localities will soon follow.

She's got the look!

Summons: An order to appear in court

Modesty: Decency or propriety in appearance

Manufacturers of pet clothing are hopeful as well. Most pet stores now have an extensive collection of fashionable outfits for dogs, and the selection is expanding every year. A smaller selection of clothing for cats is now available, too, and gear for rodents and reptiles can't be far behind. At this point, however, options for farm and zoo animals are lagging behind, with supporters left to craft their own solutions in those cases.

Of course, not everyone agrees with the animal **modesty** movement. Author Judi Barrett has published a bestselling book,

Animals Should Definitely Not Wear Clothing, which denounces the entire idea. Her position is that attempting to clothe animals is simply impractical. "Pigs will just get their outfits dirty, and goats might try to eat their shirts," she says. "Plus, can you imagine how difficult it would be for hens to lay eggs if they were forced to wear trousers?" Barrett admitted that even she allowed her dog to wear a coat on very cold days, but she maintains that animals wearing clothing should never be mandated by law.

What do you think: Should Rover's owners be required to keep his private parts under wraps? Should Mittens—and her kittens—be made to get a modesty makeover? One thing is for sure . . . until they do, avoiding any unwanted exposure will be up to you. Avert your eyes, please. Just look away!

Try It—Find Your Own Weird Law!

Are there any strange laws on the books near you? You might be surprised! Try visiting your town hall or the county clerk's office, interviewing city officials, and/or asking a local reference librarian or historian, then see what you can discover. Maybe you can even start a movement to get the law changed . . . unless you decide you'd rather keep it around just for the fun of it!

IT'S ALMOST TOO MUCH to contain within one chapter: Dogs as mayors! Trees under arrest! Societies against bare-bottomed animals! What is this world coming to?! It's times like these, my friends, when one realizes that life is a lot more interesting than we ever suspected.

But you know the drill, so start marching! One of these stories is a fake. Lean in close and whisper your guess. We promise we won't tell a soul.

A. PLEASE PLAY WITH YOUR FOOD!

Food is for eating; everyone knows that. But don't you sometimes get the urge to . . . well, *throw* your food at someone? Wait—you don't? Um, well, we don't either. Of course not.

Okay, maybe we do. Let's just agree that it's one of those urges that comes over a peaceful diner from time to time. If this happens to you on the last Wednesday of August, and you are anywhere near Valencia, Spain, then you are in luck.

Welcome to La Tomatina, the incarnation of all your

squishy-tomato-food-fight-festival dreams.

For over 70 years, a most unusual custom has developed in Buñol—a small town in the east of Spain, to which many thousands now flock every year in hopes of joining in the fun. Are you ready to get started? First, some rules. Here's what the city council has to say:

* *Only* tomatoes may be thrown. (No rogue apples allowed.)

* Squish before you toss, please. (Safety concern, or for maximum splatage?)

* Make way for the tomato trucks. (Beep beep!)

* When the water cannon says it's over, it's over. (Yes, that means *you*.)

Mayhem in the streets!

SPAIN

Valencia

They don't call it the world's biggest food fight for nothing. Before 2013, incoming crowds during the festival would swell this 9,000-person town up to 50,000 people! But safety concerns prompted the local government to get involved. You now need a ticket to attend La Tomatina, and attendance is capped at around 20,000. (The festival has been so successful, in fact, that copycat events are held from Colombia to Costa Rica to Colorado!)

Just picture the scene. Buñol town square, circa 11 a.m. Thousands of bodies are jammed into the streets, standing side by side. Make way: IT'S THE TOMATO TRUCKS! Piles upon piles of cheap, overripe fruit are heaped up. But wait—wait for it—wait for—

BOOM go the water cannons. And it's ON.

There are tomatoes *everywhere.* Ooey, gooey, smooshed tomatoes. Over 220,000 pounds of super-ripe fruit, oozing rivers of juice and pulp everywhere. Everyone in sight is throwing, tossing, smashing, squashing. It's a tomato-hurling hullabaloo!

Finally, after about an hour, the food frenzy starts to slow. The water cannons fire the second time, and the fun is over. Pulp-covered fighters make their way in search of showers, garden hoses, or local rivers for a much-needed cleanse.

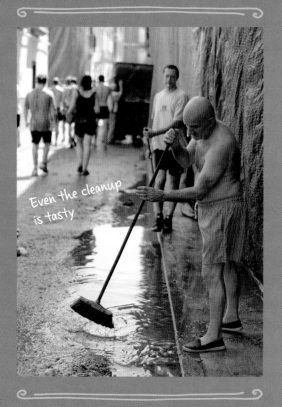

Even the cleanup is tasty

But that's not quite the end. I mean, think about it. It's like the whole town square accidentally fell inside a pot of spaghetti sauce! Luckily, fire trucks are at the ready, with their hoses a-squirting. High-pressured water gushes all over the square. Every bit of tomato goo is washed right down the drains. Not only that, but the natural acidity in the tomatoes actually disinfects and leaves the square cleaner than before. (Now that's what we'd call a win-win.)

Which is just as well, because next year, the last Wednesday in August will find tens of thousands of festivalgoers winding up their throwing arms, ready to do it all over again.

Try It—Design Your Own Festival!

If you look into the history of almost any festival, you'll often find that it started with one person and an unusual idea. And, somehow, that random event took shape into a yearly tradition that goes on to be enjoyed by people year after year!

What if you could design your ideal festival? Some points to ponder:

1. What kind of festival would it be?

2. Where would it be held?

3. How long would it last?

4. What traditions, ceremonies, or special events would it have?

5. What would it be called?

If you think you've got a winner, why not go a step further: draw posters, write press releases, make it happen. Who knows? Maybe you can bring a whole new tradition to life. At the very least, you'll have a lot of fun planning it!

B. OUT IN THE MEADOW, WHERE THE MARSHMALLOWS GROW

It's great to have something you can always count on to make your day better. Something like, say, marshmallows. These pillowy white treats are great for making s'mores, not to mention eating straight out of the package. When this glorious goodie first came into existence in the 1800s, it was made by whipping the sap from the mallow plant together with egg whites and sugar. Hello, marshmallow! Nowadays, commercial marshmallows are usually made using gelatin, but the plant-based form is seeing a whole new resurgence from a

Raw marshmallows!

most unlikely (to some people!) source: the fields of rural Iceland.

As one of the most isolated countries on Earth, the island nation of Iceland has long relied on **agriculture** as a key means of feeding its inhabitants. Local farmers make good use of the long-daylight days of summer to grow not only edible foods—potatoes, carrots, cabbages, and more—but also **fodder** crops like barley, rye, and . . . grass. Yep, grass. Or, as it is better known once it's dried, hay.

What's so special about hay, you ask? And what does it have to do with marshmallows? Here's the thing. Most harvesters the world over cut their hay off at the base. The stalk itself, after all, is what will feed their livestock. However, back in the early 1900s it was discovered that a unique soil combination gives Icelandic wild grasses an exceptionally fat and tender root. It turned

Agriculture: Farming

Fodder: Food for animals

Combine: Machine for harvesting grain crops

out that those roots were very similar to the mallow plant—except 50 times more concentrated!

Very quickly, special **combines** were designed that would pull the grass up by its roots rather than chopping it off at the base. The hay is then bundled in rounded heaps to dry, with the roots on top. Those roots are lopped off and used to make . . . marshmallows! Because the weather in Iceland is frequently cool and rainy, great white tarps are thrown over the hay bales. This is a clever nod to what has become Iceland's greatest export: the humble marshmallow.

It's important to note that those big pillowy drifts scattered across Iceland's fields are not actually giant marshmallows. (Oh, the dream!) But the roots gathered from just one of those hay bales can make enough marshmallows to fill a three-story building. Hundreds of thousands of them! With this kind of cheap (and flavorful) sap available, Icelandic marshmallow exports

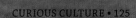

Impressive Icelandic Information

Can you guess which one of these facts about Iceland isn't true? Yes, there's only one here that isn't real!

1. The Icelandic language is essentially unchanged over the last 1,000 years.

2. Icelanders often go swimming outdoors in below-freezing temperatures.

3. Chocolate is strictly rationed and residents can be fined for consuming too much.

4. A majority of Icelandic people believe in elves.

5. In December, sunrise comes not long before noon.

6. One in ten Icelandic children will grow up to be an author.

7. Iceland does not have an army.

8. Unusual baby names have to be approved by a government committee.

9. Owning a pet turtle is illegal.

10. Raw puffin heart is a culinary delicacy.

have skyrocketed, with local candymakers crafting elaborate specialty flavors. There's even a marshmallow festival held every year in early May, where locals outdo themselves to produce the most delicious mallows. Arctic thyme-maple? Pink rutabaga molasses? Whipped blueberry meringue? Check, check, and check.

So that's the story of the Icelandic marshmallow craze, and how a humble grass launched a booming industry that is revolutionizing this quiet country. So if you're feeling that marshmallow craving, don't hesitate to pop over to Iceland for a sampling. Unless you already live there. In which case: look me up! I've got a terrific new flavor idea.

HERE, HYENA-HYENA-HYENA!

If someone asked you right now, "What do you want to be when you grow up?," a lot of things might come to your mind. A firefighter, for example. A teacher. Maybe a chocolate taster. (That's a real job!) But how many people do you suppose would answer, "Someone who feeds bloodthirsty wild animals"?

It's time for you to meet to the "hyena men" of Harar.

First, a few pertinent pointers about our good friend the hyena: it is one of the fiercest predators on Earth. A typical specimen boasts over 100 pounds of bone-crushing force, with running speeds of 40 miles per hour and super-keen senses of smell, sight, and hearing. They are infamous for consuming *all* of their prey—not just the meat, but every last bone, too. (Gulp.)

Okay, so, definitely not your lovable pet pooch. But in many places on the African

Fierce, wild, and HUNGRY

continent, hyenas are edging into everyday life—and we're not just talking about wild creatures ranging across the **savanna** looking for wounded prey to dispatch with their hungry jaws. Increasingly, packs of hyenas are moving into **urban** settings. The Ethiopian capital city of Addis Ababa, for example, is home to up to 1,000 hyenas, which scavenge from trash heaps and prey on unattended farm animals and pets.

With this growing threat, what is a concerned citizen to do? One group of people has found a solution. Let's shift our lens to the east a little, to the walled city of Harar. This hilltop city has been around for centuries, but these days Harar is known in countries around the world as the home of the hyena feeders. Say . . . what?

The story goes that, during a time of great famine several

Walled city of Harar

hundred years ago, hyenas started coming into the city and attacking livestock *and* people— and eating them! Desperate local elders came up with a solution: **porridge**. Yep—certain

Savanna: Wild, grassy plain with few trees

Urban: Referring to a city, an area where a lot of people live

Porridge: Hot cereal, such as oatmeal

volunteers began to set out porridge to feed the hyenas, in hopes of keeping them away from local residents. (Some sources say that this porridge had lots of rich butter in it, which this author feels completely explains why the hyenas may have stopped attacking.)

The porridge custom fell away after a bit. But the hyena threat lingered. So in the 1950s, a farmer got a bright idea. Remember, Harar is a city surrounded by stone walls. If they could keep the hyenas from sneaking inside those walls, the city would be safe. And so this farmer began venturing outside the city, armed with scraps of raw meat. Gather round, all you hyenas! Munch, crunch . . . success.

And so, a new profession was born.

Today, this feeding is a bona fide cultural custom, with "hyena men" delivering the nightly dinner parties (so to speak). It's even become a tourist spectacle, with visitors from overseas paying to come along on the expeditions for a chance to see these brutal predators in action.

Watch your fingers!

Make no mistake, the hyenas of Harar are nowhere near **domesticated**; anyone who has ever watched them savagely tear apart a chunk of flesh will attest to this. (Seriously. Keep waaaaay back.) But the hyena men take to their task with pride and skill. They call to individual hyenas, even giving some of them names. And the results? Nearby towns still regularly suffer vicious hyena attacks, but not Harar. They have found a way to live in peace with the animals.

Domesticated: Tame, kept as pets

This still isn't a pack you'll want to be running with any time in the near future. But it's nice to know that, sometimes, all it takes to stop a cycle of horrible violence is a trip outside the wall, some raw meat, and a person brave enough to connect the two.

Talk It Out: The More Things Change . . .

One of the fun and interesting things to do with history is compare it with the present day. Some things have stayed unchanging throughout many centuries. Others, not so much. For an interesting group discussion project, look up the history of your town, community, or school. When was it established? What was the surrounding area like? What things have changed since that time? What has stayed the same? Comparing how land, customs, and people have evolved over the years can make for a fascinating discussion (or personal project)!

Bonus assignment: Draw a "Then and Now" map for side-by-side comparison. Or dig up old photos. Seeing what is still the same might be just as amazing as noticing what has changed!

ISN'T THE WORLD AROUND us astonishing? We're talking about tomato food fights, fields full of Icelandic marshmallows, and people hand-feeding bloodthirsty predators. But only two of these three stories are true. You know what to do: Research up, and the answer will be plain as day. Off you go!

You haven't looked at the answers already, have you? We hope not! We're betting you can probably figure out the truth yourself, and isn't that more fun anyway? (And if you *have* already peeked at the answers, that's okay, too. Just keep these suggestions in mind next time you're not sure whether something you read is true or false.)

To help in your fact-finding endeavors, here are some of our best tips and tricks.

First off, we know what you're thinking: research is all about using the internet, right? That's *sort of* true. We did most of our research for this book without ever leaving home, thanks to online resources! So we're the first to admit that the internet makes doing research easier in many ways. But in other ways, it also makes it harder. You *can* find almost anything on the internet . . . but that doesn't always mean that what you find is true. In fact, sometimes people post fake stories on the internet—on purpose!—just to see if they can trick people.

So, how can YOU avoid getting fooled? It's really not that difficult.

Question everything: First and foremost, always maintain a healthy dose of skepticism. If you've learned anything from reading this book, we hope it's that you can't believe everything you read (or see in photos). It's up to you to think critically about all the things you hear, see, and read every day. Does something sound too good to be true? Maybe it is. Could someone be trying to manipulate you into doing something? Watch out! Compare the things you read with what you already know to be true—and not true—and see how this new information fits. Our advice when you find something and you're not sure whether to believe it? Don't! At least not until you've done your own research and can be reasonably sure that it's true. (See below for more on that.)

Search wisely: Internet search engines—such as Google—are great starting points, but use them with care. Search engines sort their results by what's most popular, *not* by their level of truthfulness. In fact, sometimes a well-known hoax might be the first (or most often clicked on) link you'll encounter. (Trust us, we know hoaxes!)

So, make sure you only click on links from a trusted source, such as an established newspaper or magazine, a respected university, a well-known museum, a government agency, etc. Take note of when the information was posted and who wrote it. How does the author know the information they're posting? Did they experience it themselves? Do they reveal their sources?

Finally, try to verify any questionable facts with at least two other reputable sources—and make sure they're not all referencing the same original source. If several reliable sources all provide the same information based on their own unique research, then you can feel fairly safe believing them.

Be Wiki-aware: Another popular place to begin a research project is Wikipedia. It's true that it can be a great place to *start* your research on a given subject, but you should never stop there. Remember: Wikipedia articles can be edited *by anyone at any time*. Most of the information you'll find there is probably true—but you can never be sure.

The easiest way to check the information on Wikipedia is by going straight to the sources. Most articles have footnotes that link to a section at the end of the article called References. There, you will find which online articles, books, journals, magazines, and other sources the authors used as reference material when they wrote the article. Make sure you explore those references yourself (and even those references' references!). Follow the trail to make sure the original sources are reliable, using the same tips we listed above.

Don't skip the sources: As with Wikipedia, always check through any sources provided for anything you're researching (including the stories in this book!). If no sources are listed, that should be a big red flag: Beware! If there are sources listed, do they seem reliable? Are they relevant to the topic at hand? Whenever something seems unbelievable or even a bit iffy, your first question should always be "What sources did the author use to find this information?" If you don't trust the sources, don't trust the results.

Ask the experts: One of the best ways to research is by interviewing people who know about the topic firsthand. Can you talk to someone who has relevant knowledge or experience? Yes, *you* can be an interviewer, just like we were. Don't be shy: most people will be glad you asked!

Love your librarian: Do you think libraries are a thing of the past, now that so much information is online? That couldn't be further from the truth. Your library gives you access to books, magazines, newspapers, and online databases with all sorts of scholarly articles, historical newspapers, old magazine features, and more. We couldn't write books like this if it weren't for libraries and the reference librarians who work in them. If you've got a question—any question—step right up and ask a librarian for help! That's exactly what they're there for, and they are pros.

We hope you can use these suggestions to figure out which stories in this book, as well as anywhere else you find them, are true . . . and which ones are flat-out fakes. If you find you're still not sure about any of ours, however, just read on for answers and explanations.

PART 1: HAZY HISTORIES

CHAPTER 1: OVER 1,000 YEARS AGO

The past is not only distant, but sometimes murky, too. Did you guess that "Mammoth Cave's Mystery Walker" was a fake? If so, you are correct. Mammoth Cave, and all the facts about it, are as true as can be—but the Mystery Walker is pure cave-loving fantasy. However, we stand by our passionate love for caves (well, one of us does, anyway). They are just as full of mystery and adventure as you could possibly imagine. Go find some caves today!

Better Off Buried—Or Not!

Three upright oak doors, all in a row, have not (to our knowledge) been discovered buried underground. But oh gracious, wouldn't that make a great story opener?

CHAPTER 2: OVER 100 YEARS AGO

The odd "man" out in this collection is none other than the patriotic and well-crafted Boilerplate. While this machine of mystery never existed in real life, its legend is strong and well worth investigating further. The fictional creation of Paul Guinan and Anina Bennett, Boilerplate and his adventures can be explored further in the book *Boilerplate: History's Mechanical Marvel*, which gives a fresh and fascinating (if not entirely factual) twist on events of recent history.

Written in Stone

Wacky inscriptions, like whoa! The made-up one here is "Died as she lived: with sharpened pencil always in hand." If there is a Laurel Morton out there reading this, we trust that she is alive and well. (Seriously, though. Watch out for those sharp pencils.)

CHAPTER 3: OVER 10 YEARS AGO

This was a bit of a tricky one. The ship of cannibal rats *was* a popular rumor on the internet a few years ago, and many of the facts given in that story are actually true. The *Lyubov Orlova* was really adrift at sea for a couple of months, although it was most likely completely deserted. Any rats present probably died of dehydration pretty quickly on their unfortunate voyage, without becoming cannibalistic or insane. And they're no longer a problem in any case, because the ship is believed to have sunk in early 2013. (Yes, we also fudged the dates a little!)

Games People Played

What a riot of games! Maybe we can start a new-old-games trend? In any case, the fake here is Lig-a-Lag. But that's not to say it has to *stay* a fake. Anybody want to make up a new game?

CHAPTER 4: NATURAL

Here's how you know a story is a good one: The author who did *not* write and research "Magical Mankato" didn't realize that it was a fake until the book was completely finished! Somehow, she had been reading her coauthor's work as being true the whole time. Incorrect! Mankato, Minnesota, is just as weather-flexible as the rest of Minnesota, for better or for worse. But we're sure it's still a nice place to visit.

Geological Wonders

With so many wild and wacky names, we don't blame you at all for not guessing the incorrect one. To set the record straight, though, the fake here is Ziggyzag Geyser. (Too bad, right? We liked that one.)

CHAPTER 5: UNNATURAL

After reading this chapter, are you ready to say good-bye to your family dog and send them away to Dog Island? We sure hope not! Dog Island is NOT a real place, and we're pretty sure your dog would prefer to stay right where they are, in a comfortable house with loads of human caring and companionship. If not, then perhaps you better start pampering that pooch a bit more! Biscuits and belly rubs, anyone? And you should probably start by apologizing for even considering sending them away in the first place.

A Menagerie of Micronations

The fake country on this list is none other than Queen's Basin. Which, we might add, is a bit of indulgence on the part of your authors: It is in fact a "real" fictional country, from Ammi-Joan Paquette's Princess Juniper series. A pretty cool story about setting up a micronation, if you ask us.

CHAPTER 6: SUPERNATURAL

You guessed this one, didn't you? Yep, the hoax in this chapter is "Everybody Smile and Say 'Fairies'!" It's a tricky one, though. The events itself—the cousins, their reported sighting, and the surrounding hullabaloo, including Sir Arthur Conan Doyle's involvement—all happened just as we described it. And for many years, the girls stuck to their story. But much later in life, the truth finally came out: there were no fairy sightings. The photos themselves were real—but the creatures were just paper cutouts. Apparently, the girls were originally having a bit of fun, until things spun out of control. Oh, what a tangled web we weave. . . .

Strange but (Mostly) True Cemetery Facts

The fake on this list is La Recoleta's pet cemetery. La Recoleta did become famous, however, for its many living feline residents and the woman who cared for them.

CHAPTER 7: INTERESTING INDIVIDUALS

Of the three stories in this section, the fabricated one is "My, Oh My, Magnetism!" The human body does give off a small amount of electrical energy, and biomagnetism—the phenomenon of magnetic fields that are produced by living things—is a legitimate thing. But these fields are extremely weak, and nothing like the case of Antonia Varga has ever been recorded. Or at least—it hasn't *yet*. Don't be too quick to hang up your superhero cape; you never know. . . .

Is That Really a Thing?!

Of all these way-out-there inventions, the one that does not actually exist is the hula-hooper. And if you guessed that correctly, you deserve a medal!

CHAPTER 8: LAW AND ORDER

This one is another tricky one, with partial truths stretched just enough to make it undeniably false. Comedian Alan Abel really did announce the formation of the Society for Indecency to Naked Animals (SINA) in the early 1960s, but the whole thing was a hoax. He did happen to get some legitimate supporters, but he never accepted any donations nor (as far as we know) was any legislation ever effected by the society's efforts. We highly recommend you take a look at *Animals Should Definitely Not Wear Clothing*, by Judi and Ron Barrett, though: it's a fun read! (The quote we attributed to her is entirely made up.)

Lawbreakers Beware!

Aren't you glad you know about all these illegal activities? The one on this list you do *not* need to worry about is running in pitch-darkness. Whether in South Africa, or anywhere else (to our knowledge), you are safe from the law. But not from bumping into random stuff, so . . . be careful.

CHAPTER 9: CURIOUS CULTURE

As soon as we saw photos of those lovely marshmallow-like hay bales lying in their Icelandic fields, we knew this was a hoax worth crafting. Alas, "Out in the Pasture, Where the Marshmallows Grow" is pure fiction—the marshmallow side of it, anyway. The hay bales are real, and the country of Iceland is too, of course. Quite honestly, though, someone should start a marshmallow festival. Some of our invented flavors are sure to be *gold*!

Impressive Icelandic Information

Iceland is a very cool country, with some spectacular customs. The one on this list you do not need to worry about, however, is chocolate consumption. Chocolate in Iceland is not rationed in the least, and there are no fines given for overconsumption. (You can still get a stomachache, though.)

BIBLIOGRAPHY

PART 1: HAZY HISTORIES

CHAPTER 1: OVER 1,000 YEARS AGO
Mammoth Cave's Mystery Walker

Crawford, Matthew M., Richard A. Olson, Richard S. Toomey III, and Lillian J. Scoggins. "Geology of Mammoth Cave National Park, Kentucky." Map. University of Kentucky. Accessed April 30, 2017. http://kgs.uky.edu/kgsweb/olops/pub/kgs/mcs186_12.pdf.

"Fossil Footprints." Genesis Park Fossil Footprints Comments. Accessed April 30, 2017. www.genesispark.com/exhibits/evidence/paleontological/footprints/.

"Geologic Formations." National Parks Service. Accessed April 30, 2017. www.nps.gov/maca/learn/nature/geologicformations.htm.

Livesay, Ann. *Geology of the Mammoth Cave National Park Area*. Lexington: University of Kentucky, 1953. http://kgs.uky.edu/kgsweb/olops/pub/kgs/XSP7reduce.pdf.

"Mammoth Cave National Park." National Parks Service. Accessed May 31, 2017. www.nps.gov/maca/index.htm.

"Mammoth Cave Online." Accessed April 30, 2017. http://mammothcave.com.

Shetler, Scott. "Inside the Wild World of Mammoth Cave National Park." Quirky Travel Guy. May 12, 2014. http://quirkytravelguy.com/longest-cave-system-mammoth-cave-national-park.

Holey Molars!

Laskow, Sarah. "Found: A 13,000-Year-Old Dental Filling Made of Bitumen." Atlas Obscura. April 11, 2017. www.atlasobscura.com/articles/earliest-cavity-filling-in-history.

Oxilia, Gregorio, Marco Peresani, Matteo Romandini, Chiara Matteucci, Cynthianne Debono Spiteri, Amanda G. Henry, Dieter Schulz, et al. "Earliest Evidence of Dental Caries Manipulation in the Late Upper Palaeolithic." Scientific Reports 5, no. 1 (2015). doi:10.1038/srep12150.

Scharping, Nathaniel. "13,000-Year-Old Fillings Prove Ancient Dentistry Was Brutal." *Discover* (blog). April 10, 2017. http://blogs.discovermagazine.com/d-brief/2017/04/10/ancient-dentistry-tooth-filling/#.WOve_VMrLUI.

A Curse on All Thieving Bathers

Adams, Geoff W. "The Social and Cultural Implications of Curse Tablets [defixiones] in Britain and on the Continent." Accessed May 1, 2017. www.ut.ee/klassik/sht/2006/adams2.pdf.

"Curse Tablets from Roman Britain: Archaeological Sites." Accessed May 1, 2017. http://curses.csad.ox.ac.uk/sites/index.shtml.

Fagan, Garrett G. *Bathing in Public in the Roman World*. Ann Arbor: University of Michigan Press, 2002.

Flint, Valerie et al. *Witchcraft and Magic in Europe: Ancient Greece and Rome*. Vol. 2. London: Athlone, 1999.

Gager, John G. *Curse Tablets and Binding Spells from the Ancient World*. Oxford University Press, 1992.

"Key Objects of the Collection." The Roman Baths. November 21, 2016. www.romanbaths.co.uk/key-objects-collection.

Revell, Louise. "Religion and Ritual in the Western Provinces." *Greece and Rome* 54, no. 2 (2007): 220–22.

Wilson, Roger John Anthony. *A Guide to the Roman Remains in Britain*. London: Constable, 2002.

CHAPTER 2: OVER 100 YEARS AGO

Onesimus and the Fight against Smallpox

"Frequently Asked Questions and Answers on Smallpox." World Health Organization. June 28, 2016. www.who.int/csr/disease/smallpox/faq/en.

Niven, Steven J. "Onesimus (fl. 1706–1717), Slave and Medical Pioneer, Was Born in The . . ." Hutchins Center. Accessed April 13, 2017. http://hutchinscenter.fas.harvard.edu/onesimus-fl-1706-1717-slave-and-medical-pioneer-was-born.

"Smallpox." Centers for Disease Control and Prevention. August 30, 2016. www.cdc.gov/smallpox/history/history.html.

Widmer, Ted. "How an African Slave Helped Boston Fight Smallpox." BostonGlobe.com. October 17, 2014. www.bostonglobe.com/ideas/2014/10/17/how-african-slave-helped-boston-fight-smallpox/XFhsMMvTGCeV62YP0XhhZI/story.html.

All Aboard the Railway of the Dead

Brandon, David, and Alan Brooke. *London: City of the Dead.* Stroud, England: History, 2008.

"The Cemetery Railway." The Cemetery Railway. Accessed June 7, 2017. www.tbcs.org.uk/cemetery_railway.html.

Clarke, John M. "Demise of the Necropolis Railway." Accessed May 2, 2017. www.john-clarke.co.uk/demise.html.

"London Necropolis Railway." Transport Trust. Accessed May 2, 2017. www.transporttrust.com/heritage-sites/heritage-detail/london-necropolis-railway.

Ruggeri, Amanda. "Autos—The Passenger Train Created to Carry the Dead." BBC. October 18, 2016. www.bbc.com/autos/story/20161018-the-passenger-train-that-carried-the-dead.

Slade, Paul. "Paul Slade—Journalist." PlanetSlade.com. Accessed June 7, 2017. www.planetslade.com/necropolis-railway1.html.

Boilerplate: The Man, the Myth, the Machine

"AITopics." A Brief History of AI. Accessed May 3, 2017. https://aitopics.org/misc/brief-history.

Guinan, Paul, and Anina Bennett. "Boilerplate as Soldier." The Victorian Robot in Combat. Accessed May 3, 2017. http://timetunnel.bigredhair.com/boilerplate/soldier/index.html.

———. "Boilerplate: Mechanical Marvel of the Nineteenth Century." Boilerplate: History of a Victorian Era Robot. Accessed May 3, 2017. http://timetunnel.bigredhair.com/boilerplate/intro.html.

———. "Boilerplate Unveiled." Boilerplate at the World's Columbian Exposition. Accessed May 3, 2017. http://timetunnel.bigredhair.com/boilerplate/bp.unveiled.html.

———. "See Inside." Big Red Hair. Accessed May 3, 2017. www.bigredhair.com/books/boilerplate/see-inside.

———. "Timeline." Big Red Hair. Accessed May 3, 2017. www.bigredhair.com/books/boilerplate/timeline.

Isom, James. "A Brief History of Robotics." MegaGiant Robotics. Accessed May 3, 2017. http://robotics.megagiant.com/history.html.

CHAPTER 3: OVER 10 YEARS AGO

Audubon the ~~Painter~~ Prankster

Cherrix, Kira. "A Fishy Tail." Field Book Project. April 1, 2014. http://nmnh.typepad.com/fieldbooks/2014/04/a-fishy-tail.html.

Daley, Jason. "Audubon Pranked Fellow Naturalist by Making Up Fake Rodents." Smithsonian.com. April 27, 2016. www.smithsonianmag.com/smart-news/audubon-pranked-fellow-naturalist-making-fake-rodents-180958907.

Flood, Alison. "John James Audubon and the Natural History of a Hoax." Guardian. May 3, 2016. www.theguardian.com/books/booksblog/2016/may/03/john-james-audubon-and-the-natural-history-of-a-hoax.

Horowitz, Kate. "John James Audubon's Made-Up Bulletproof Fish." Mental Floss. December 10, 2015. http://mentalfloss.com/article/72339/john-james-audubons-made-bulletproof-fish.

Langston, Erica. "Birder, Painter, Troll, and Trickster—The Secret Life of John James Audubon." Audubon. July 22, 2016. www.audubon.org/news/birder-painter-troll-and-trickster-secret-life-john-james-audubon.

Laskow, Sarah. "Audubon Made Up at Least 28 Fake Species to Prank a Rival." Atlas Obscura. February 22, 2017. www.atlasobscura.com/articles/audubon-made-up-at-least-28-fake-species-to-prank-a-rival.

Markle, Douglas F. "Audubon's Hoax: Ohio River Fishes Described by Rafinesque." *Archives of Natural History* 24, no. 3 (1997): 439–47. www.euppublishing.com/doi/abs/10.3366/anh.1997.24.3.439.

Woodman, Neal. "Pranked by Audubon: Constantine S. Rafinesque's Description of John James Audubon's Imaginary Kentucky Mammals." *Archives of Natural History* 43, no. 1 (2016): 95–108. https://repository.si.edu/bitstream/handle/10088/28626/2016%20Pranked%20by%20Audubon.pdf?sequence=1&isAllowed=y.

Cannibal Rats, Ahoy!

Bellini, Jarrett. "Apparently This Matters: A Ghost Ship with Cannibal Rats." CNN. January 27, 2014. www.cnn.com/2014/01/24/tech/web/apparently-this-matters-lyubov-orlova-ghost-ship.

Guilford, Gwynn. "How a 1,500-Ton Ocean Liner Turns into a Cannibal-Rat-Infested Ghost Ship." Quartz. January 23, 2014. https://qz.com/169990/how-a-1500-ton-ocean-liner-turns-into-a-cannibal-rat-infested-ghost-ship.

Harding, Nick. "Ship of Ghouls: Liner Adrift for 12 Months and Heading to UK." *Sun*. April 5, 2016. www.thesun.co.uk/archives/news/528110/ship-of-ghouls.

Layne, Ken. "Abandoned Cruise Ship Full of Starving Rats Headed For Land." Gawker. January 23, 2014. http://gawker.com/abandoned-cruise-ship-full-of-starving-rats-headed-for-1507439976.

Prynne, Miranda. "Ghost Ship Carrying Cannibal Rats Could Be Heading for Britain." *Telegraph*. January 23, 2014. www.telegraph.co.uk/news/uknews/10591704/Ghost-ship-carrying-cannibal-rats-could-be-heading-for-Britain.html.

Richards, Chris. "Ghost Ship Crewed Only by Cannibal Rats Feared to Be Heading for Scottish Coast." *Daily Record*. January 23, 2014. www.dailyrecord.co.uk/news/weird-news/ghost-ship-crewed-cannibal-rats-3053164.

Tomlinson, Simon. "Could This Russian Ghost Ship Infested with Cannibal Rats Beach in Britain? Experts Fear Storms Have Driven Abandoned Cruise Liner towards Land after Canadian Tow Ship Lost It a Year Ago." Daily Mail Online. January 23, 2014. www.dailymail.co.uk/news/article-2544444/Russian-ghost-ship-infested-CANNIBAL-RATS-beach-Britain-going-missing-Atlantic.html.

Withnall, Adam. "Lyubov Orlova: Ghost Ship Carrying Cannibal Rats 'Could Be Heading for Britain.'" *Independent*. January 23, 2014. www.independent.co.uk/news/uk/home-news/mystery-of-the-lyubov-orlova-ghost-ship-full-of-cannibal-rats-could-be-heading-for-british-coast-9080103.html.

The North American Santa Accident

Bailey, Chelsea, and Associated Press. "Here Comes Santa: The Adorable Origins of NORAD's Santa Tracker." NBCNews.com. December 24, 2016. www.nbcnews.com/news/us-news/here-comes-santa-claus-norad-tracks-santa-more-60-years-n699821.

Garber, Megan. "Updated: NORAD Tracks Santa's Path on Christmas Eve Because of a Typo." Atlantic.com December 16, 2013. www.theatlantic.com/technology/archive/2013/12/norad-tracks-santas-path-on-christmas-eve-because-of-a-typo/282388.

"NORAD Tracks Santa." Accessed April 24, 2017. www.norad.mil/About-NORAD/NORAD-Tracks-Santa.

NPR. "NORAD's Santa Tracker Began with a Typo and a Good Sport." December 19, 2014. www.npr.org/2014/12/19/371647099/norads-santa-tracker-began-with-a-typo-and-a-good-sport.

PART 2: PECULIAR PLACES

CHAPTER 4: NATURAL

Magical Mankato

"Let's 'Make It in Mankato.'" Mankato, MN Home Page. Accessed April 24, 2017. http://descy.50megs.com/Emankato/mankato.html.

National Geographic Society. "Geyser." October 9, 2012. www.nationalgeographic.org/encyclopedia/geyser.

"Thermal Springs List for the United States." Accessed April 27, 2017. www.ngdc.noaa.gov/nndc/struts/results?op_0=eq&v_0=&op_1=l&v_1=&op_2=l&v_2=&t=100006&s=1&d=1.

"Visit Greater Mankato Minnesota | It's All So Close!" Visit Mankato. March 21, 2016. http://visitgreatermankato.com.

"Visitor Information." Mankato, MN. Accessed April 25, 2017. www.mankatomn.gov/about-mankato/visitor-information.

Are You Smarter Than a Bird Brain?

"Exhibits." Accessed May 5, 2017. www3.uca.edu/iqzoo/Exhibits/exhibits.htm.

Gillaspy, J. Arthur, Jr., and Elson M. Bihm. "Keller Bramwell Breland (1915–1965)." Encyclopedia of Arkansas History and Culture. July 16, 2007. www.encyclopediaofarkansas.net/encyclopedia/entry-detail.aspx?search=1&entryID=2530.

Hough, Christopher. "IQ Zoo." Encyclopedia of Arkansas History and Culture. October 10, 2013. www.encyclopediaofarkansas.net/encyclopedia/entry-detail.aspx?entryID=2538.

Joyce, Nick, and David B. Baker. "The IQ Zoo." *Monitor on Psychology* 39, no. 8 (September 2008): 24. www.apa.org/monitor/2008/09/animals.aspx.

Marr, John N. "Marian Breland Bailey: The Mouse Who Reinforced." *Arkansas Historical Quarterly* 61, no. 1 (2002): 59. doi:10.2307/40031038.

"Science: I.Q. Zoo." *Time*. February 28, 1955. http://content.time.com/time/subscriber/article/0,33009,861239,00.html.

Skinner, B. F. "Definition." The B. F. Skinner Foundation. February 28, 2014. www.bfskinner.org/behavioral-science/definition.

Vanderbilt, Tom. "The CIA's Most Highly-Trained Spies Weren't Even Human." Smithsonian.com. October 1, 2013. www.smithsonianmag.com/history/the-cias-most-highly-trained-spies-werent-even-human-20149/?all.

Winters, Emily. "What Is the IQ Zoo?" Cummings Center for the History of Psychology. 2013. www.uakron.edu/chp/abe/the-iq-zoo.

Wright, Andy. "The Experimental Zoo Where Parrots Rollerskated and Chickens Played Baseball." Atlas Obscura. March 10, 2017. www.atlasobscura.com/articles/iq-zoo-arkansas.

Yin, Sophia. "The Best Animal Trainers in History: Interview with Bob and Marian Bailey, Part 1." August 13, 2012. https://drsophiayin.com/blog/entry/the-best-animal-trainers-in-history-interview-with-bob-and-marian-bailey.

———. "The Best Animal Trainers in History: Interview with Bob and Marian Bailey, Part 2." August 17, 2012. https://drsophiayin.com/blog/entry/the-best-animal-trainers-in-history-interview-with-bob-and-marian-bailey-2.

Honey: So Sweet and So . . . Colorful?

Alexander, Lisa. "17 Top-Rated Alsace Villages and Medieval Towns." PlanetWare.com. Accessed May 6, 2017. www.planetware.com/france/alsace-route-du-vin-f-a-rovi.htm.

Andries, Kate. "Pictures: Colored Honey Made by Candy-Eating French Bees." *National Geographic*. April 7, 2016. http://news.nationalgeographic.com/news/2012/10/pictures/121011-blue-honey-honeybees-animals-science.

Hunter, Molly. "Bees Producing Blue and Green Honey: Are M&M's to Blame?" ABC News. October 4, 2012. http://abcnews.go.com/blogs/headlines/2012/10/bees-producing-blue-and-green-honey-are-mms-to-blame.

Kim, JuJu. "French Bees Produce Blue Honey." *Time*. October 5, 2012. http://newsfeed.time.com/2012/10/05/french-bees-produce-blue-honey.

Laskow, Sarah. "Why Are French Bees Making Blue and Green Honey?" Grist. October 8, 2012. http://grist.org/article/why-are-french-bees-making-blue-and-green-honey-3.

"M&M's-crazed Bees Make Blue and Green Honey." France 24. October 5, 2012. www.france24.com/en/20121004-mms-crazed-french-bees-produce-blue-green-honey-ribeauville-alsace-france.

Turnbull, Bill. "Ask a Grown-up: How Do Bees Make Honey?" *Guardian*. August 10, 2013. www.theguardian.com/lifeandstyle/2013/aug/10/how-bees-make-honey-ask-a-grown-up.

CHAPTER 5: UNNATURAL

Welcome to Molossia, Population: 6.

Chadwick, Alex. "'Lonely Planet' Explores Micronations." Transcript. NPR. November 1, 2006. www.npr.org/templates/story/story.php?storyId=6416479.

"Conference Information." MicroCon 2015. http://www.molossia.org/microcon/information2015.html.

Great Big Story. "This Man Runs a Micronation of 32 People." Performed by Kevin Baugh. May 8, 2016. https://www.youtube.com/watch?v=r2bJXGX8-dM.

Mastony, Colleen. "In the Spirit of Independence Day." *Chicago Tribune*. July 3, 2008. http://articles.chicagotribune.com/2008-07-03/features/0807010471_1_lonely-planet-declared-global-politics.

"Micronation." Oxford Living Dictionaries. Accessed May 8, 2017. https://en.oxforddictionaries .com/definition/micronation.

"Republic of Molossia—Official Website." Accessed May 8, 2017. www.molossia.org/countryeng .html.

Spencer, Luke. "Interviewing the President of the Sovereign Nation inside Nevada." Atlas Obscura. April 14, 2016. www.atlasobscura.com/articles/interviewing-the-president-of-the-sovereign-nation-inside-nevada.

Big Bird Goes to Church

"A Towering Prayer House in the Hills." *Jakarta Globe*. Accessed May 6, 2017. http://jakartaglobe.id/features/towering-prayer-house-hills.

Jauregui, Andres. "Indonesia's 'Chicken Church' Is So Much Cooler Than Florida's." Huffington Post. July 13, 2015. www.huffingtonpost.com/2015/07/13/chicken-church-indonesia-gereja-ayam_n_7785146.html.

Going to the Dogs . . . On Dog Island

"Dog Island Free Forever." Accessed May 7, 2017. www.thedogisland.com.

Statista. "Number of Dogs in the U.S., 2017 | Statistic." 2017. www.statista.com/statistics/198100/dogs-in-the-united-states-since-2000.

Thompson, Laurie Ann, and Paul Schmid. *My Dog Is the Best*. New York: Farrar, Straus and Giroux, 2015.

CHAPTER 6: SUPERNATURAL

Hello, Dolly!

Google Maps. Accessed June 8, 2017. www.google.com/maps/@33.8564802,134.0195114,3a,75y ,101h,74.99t/data=!3m6!1e1!3m4!1sHOoUvTsq_J5g5qrqExtA9w!2e0!7i13312!8i6656.

Jaffe, Ina. "A Dying Japanese Village Brought Back to Life—By Scarecrows." NPR. August 26, 2016. www.npr.org/sections/parallels/2016/08/26/490687505/a-dying-japanese-village-brought-back-to-life-by-scarecrows.

McCurry, Justin. "In Ageing Japanese Village, Dolls Take Place of Dwindling Population." *Guardian*. January 7, 2015. www.theguardian.com/world/2015/jan/07/japanese-village-dolls-ageing-population-nagoro.

Meyers, Chris. "Time Stands Still in Japan's Village of Scarecrows." Reuters. March 16, 2015. www.reuters.com/article/us-japan-dolls-wideimage-idUSKBN0MC0ME20150316.

Sim, David. "Village of the Scarecrows: Residents of Nagoro in Japan Are Being Replaced by Life-size Straw Dolls." *International Business Times UK*. December 30, 2015. www.ibtimes.co.uk/village-scarecrows-residents-nagoro-japan-are-being-replaced-by-life-size-straw-dolls-1492079.

The Valley of Dolls. Produced by Fritz Schumann. Performed by Ayano Tsukimi. Vimeo. 2014. https://vimeo.com/92453765.

Everybody Smile and Say "Fairies"

Boese, Alex. "The Cottingley Fairies." Museum of Hoaxes. Accessed May 9, 2017. http://hoaxes.org/photo_database/image/the_cottingley_fairies.

"Cottingley Fairies." Accessed June 8, 2017. www.cottingley.net/fairies.shtml.

Doyle, Arthur Conan. *The Coming of the Fairies*. New York: Samuel Weiser, 1972. https://archive.org/download/comingoffairies00doylrich/comingoffairies00doylrich.pdf.

Heydt, Bruce. "The Adventure of the Cottingley Fairies." *British Heritage*. May 2004, 20–25. https://britishheritage.com/the-adventure-of-the-cottingley-fairies.

Loxton, Jason, Jillian Baker, Jim W. W. Smith, and Daniel Loxton. "The Cottingley Fairies." *Skeptic*, 2010, 72B–81. ProQuest Research Library [ProQuest]: 89058578.

Middleton, Nicholas. "The 'Midg' Falling Plate Camera." Photo-Analogue. January 1, 1970. http://photo-analogue.blogspot.com/2015/07/the-midg-falling-plate-camera.html.

The Creepy Case of Highgate Cemetery

Beresford, Mathew. *From Demons to Dracula: The Creation of the Modern Vampire Myth*. London: Reaktion Books, 2011.

Ellis, Bill. "The Highgate Cemetery Vampire Hunt: The Anglo-American Connection in Satanic Cult Lore." *Folklore* 104, no. 1–2 (1993): 13–39.

Farrant, Della. *Haunted Highgate*. Stroud, Gloucestershire: History Press, 2014.

Guiley, Rosemary. *The Encyclopedia of Vampires, Werewolves, and Other Monsters*. New York: Checkmark Books, 2005.

"History." Highgate Cemetery. Accessed May 9, 2017. https://highgatecemetery.org/about/history.

PART 3: PERPLEXING PEOPLE

CHAPTER 7: INTERESTING INDIVIDUALS

Ben Franklin's Farts

"Founders Online: From Benjamin Franklin to the Royal Academy of Brussels . . ." National Archives and Records Administration. Accessed May 18, 2017. https://founders.archives.gov/documents/Franklin/01-32-02-0281.

Franklin, Benjamin. "Founding Era." Teaching American History. Accessed May 18, 2017. http://teachingamericanhistory.org/library/document/to-the-royal-academy-of-farting.

———. "Letter to the Royal Academy of Brussels." Early Americas Digital Archive. Accessed May 18, 2017. http://eada.lib.umd.edu/text-entries/letter-to-the-royal-academy-of-brussels.

Franklin, Benjamin, and Carl Japikse. *Fart Proudly: Writings of Benjamin Franklin You Never Read in School*. Berkeley, CA: Frog, 2003.

Reilly, Lucas. "Benjamin Franklin and Jonathan Swift Were Fart Joke Masters." Mental Floss. January 28, 2013. http://mentalfloss.com/article/48601/benjamin-franklin-and-jonathan-swift-were-fart-joke-masters.

Stromberg, Joseph. "In 1781, Benjamin Franklin Wrote an Essay about Farting." Vox. January 13, 2015. www.vox.com/2015/1/13/7533665/benjamin-frankling-farting.

The Life-Saving Magic of Tilly Smith

"Girl, 10, Used Geography Lesson to Save Lives." *Telegraph*. January 1, 2005. www.telegraph.co.uk/news/1480192/Girl-10-used-geography-lesson-to-save-lives.html.

Hornig, Jessica. "From Fear to Survival: Knowledge Is Key." ABC News. January 22, 2009. http://abcnews.go.com/2020/fear-survival-knowledge-key/story?id=6691940.

"Indian Ocean Tsunami of 2004." *Encyclopædia Britannica*. Accessed May 12, 2017. www.britannica.com/event/Indian-Ocean-tsunami-of-2004.

Owen, James. "Tsunami Family Saved by Schoolgirl's Geography Lesson." *National Geographic*. January 18, 2005. http://news.nationalgeographic.com/news/2005/01/0118_050118_tsunami_geography_lesson.html.

My, Oh My, Magnetism!

Blaustein, Michael. "Meet Magneto Boy, the Kid Who Attracts Metal with His Body." *New York Post*. November 19, 2014. http://nypost.com/2014/11/19/meet-magneto-boy-the-kid-who-attracts-metal-with-his-body.

Hoadley, Rick. "Experiments with Magnets and Our Surroundings." CoolMagnetMan. Accessed May 14, 2017. www.coolmagnetman.com/magflux.htm.

"The People Who Can't Wear Watches." The Skeptics Society Forum. 2009. www.skepticforum.com/viewtopic.php?t=11419.

Phillips, Tom. "'Human Magnet' Brenda Allison Experiencing Metal Fatigue." *Metro*. December 3, 2012. http://metro.co.uk/2010/08/20/human-magnet-brenda-allison-experiencing-metal-fatigue-485624.

Pilkington, Mark. "Strange Attractors." *Guardian*. April 28, 2004. www.theguardian.com/education/2004/apr/29/research.highereducation2.

"Q & A: How Do Magnets Work?" Ask the Van, Department of Physics, University of Illinois at Urbana-Champaign. Accessed May 14, 2017. https://van.physics.illinois.edu/qa/listing.php?id=434.

"What Are Electromagnetic Fields?" World Health Organization. Accessed May 14, 2017. www.who.int/peh-emf/about/WhatisEMF/en.

CHAPTER 8: LAW AND ORDER

When the Boss Says "Bark"

Associated Press. "Dog-gone: Canine Candidate Re-elected Minnesota Town Mayor." Minnesota Public Radio News. August 24, 2016. www.mprnews.org/story/2016/08/24/dog-wins-reelection-mayor-cormorant-township.

"Cormorant Township Board Meeting Minutes." Cormorant Township. Accessed May 18, 2017. www.cormoranttownship.org/index.asp?SEC=7B569911-EA99-4E2F-8962-D5A2029D1E16&Type=B_BASIC.

Data Access and Dissemination Systems (DADS). "Community Facts." American FactFinder. October 5, 2010. https://factfinder.census.gov/faces/nav/jsf/pages/community_facts .xhtml#.

Figalora, Sarah. "Would-Be Mayor Gracious After Losing to Dog." ABC News. August 13, 2014. http://abcnews.go.com/US/mayor-gracious-losing-dog/story?id=24961792.

Filley, Ty. "Mutt Turns Mayor in Small Town Minnesota." WDAY. August 20, 2016. www.wday .com/news/4098641-mutt-turns-mayor-small-town-minnesota.

Revesz, Rachael. "Dog Elected Mayor in Minnesota Town of Cormorant for Third Term in a Row." *Independent*. August 23, 2016. www.independent.co.uk/news/world/americas/dog-mayor-minnesota-cormorant-duke-lassie-a7205801.html.

Schoch, Al. "Duke the Dog Sworn In as Mayor of Cormorant, Minn." WCCO | CBS Minnesota. August 16, 2014. http://minnesota.cbslocal.com/2014/08/16/duke-the-dog-to-be-sworn-in-as-mayor-of-cormorant-minn.

Stop, in the Name of the Tree Police!

Abraham, Bobins. "Meanwhile in Pakistan, There Is a Banyan Tree That Has Been Under Arrest for Nearly 120 Years." Indiatimes.com. September 2, 2016. www.indiatimes.com/news/ weird/meanwhile-in-pakistan-there-is-a-banyan-tree-that-has-been-under-arrest-for-nearly-120-years-261023.html.

Butt, Shahbaz. 2016. EPaper | Dawn.com. http://epaper.dawn.com/Advt.php?StoryImage =01_09_2016_181_005.

Sindhu, Haider Ali. "This Tree Has Been Under Arrest for the Past 118 Years." *Daily Pakistan* Global. June 17, 2016. https://en.dailypakistan.com.pk/pakistan/this-tree-has-been-under-arrest-for-the-past-118-years.

Tharoor, Ishaan. "This Chained, Century-Old Tree in Pakistan Is a Perfect Metaphor for Colonialism." Washington Post. September 3, 2016. www.washingtonpost.com/news/ worldviews/wp/2016/09/03/this-chained-century-old-tree-in-pakistan-is-a-perfect-metaphor-for-colonialism.

Zia, Asad. "Colonial Rustlings: Under the Shade of the Chained Banyan Tree." *Express Tribune*. January 5, 2013. https://tribune.com.pk/story/489734/colonial-rustlings-under-the-shade-of-the-chained-banyan-tree.

A Little Decency, Please

"About · SINA—Society for Indecency to Naked Animals." Causes. Accessed May 22, 2017. www.causes.com/causes/283604-sina-society-for-indecency-to-naked-animals/about#_=_.

Barrett, Judi, and Ron Barrett. *Animals Should Definitely Not Wear Clothing.* New York: Little Simon, 2012.

Boese, Alex. "The Society for Indecency to Naked Animals." Museum of Hoaxes. Accessed May 22, 2017. http://hoaxes.org/archive/permalink/the_society_for_indecency_to_naked_animals.

Keohane, Joe. "The Life and Times of America's Greatest Hoaxer." *Slate Magazine.* February 26, 2008. www.slate.com/articles/arts/dvdextras/2008/02/would_you_like_a_hair_sandwich.html.

Washington, Glynn, and Alan Abel. "Society for Indecency to Naked Animals." NPR. March 14, 2014. www.npr.org/2014/03/14/290119435/society-for-indecency-to-naked-animals.

CHAPTER 9: CURIOUS CULTURE

Please Play with Your Food!

Cleary, Tom. "La Tomatina: 5 Fast Facts You Need to Know." Heavy.com. August 25, 2015. http://heavy.com/news/2015/08/la-tomatina-70th-anniversary-google-doodle-bunol-valencia-spain-tomatoes-food-fight-history-photos-video-squashed-2015-facts-rules.

"La Tomatina 2017 Buy OFFICIAL Tickets." Accessed May 16, 2017. www.tomatina.es/en.

"La Tomatina Festival Information, Accommodation & Tours." Accessed May 16, 2017. www.latomatinatours.com.

"La Tomatina—Tomatoe Fight in Spain." DonQuijote. Accessed May 16, 2017. www.donquijote.org/culture/spain/society/holidays/la-tomatina.

Mullins, Deirdre. "La Tomatina." RTÉ.ie. July 3, 2009. www.rte.ie/lifestyle/travel/2009/0626/141194-latomatina.

Riess, Jeanie. "Today Was the World's Biggest Food Fight, Welcome to La Tomatina." Smithsonian.com. August 29, 2012. www.smithsonianmag.com/arts-culture/today-was-the-worlds-biggest-food-fight-welcome-to-la-tomatina-18541800.

"Spanish Town Charges Fee for Tomato Fight." ABC News. August 28, 2013. www.abc.net.au/news/2013-08-28/spanish-tomato-throwing-festival-charges-fee-for-first-time/4918838.

Out in the Meadow Where the Marshmallows Grow

"Are the Bales of Hay in the Icelandic Countryside Colour Coded?" *Iceland Review*. October 14, 2011. http://icelandreview.com/stuff/ask-ir/2011/10/14/are-bales-hay-icelandic-countryside-colour-coded.

"Gigantic Marshmallows on Icelandic Farms? • R/Iceland." Reddit. 2015. www.reddit.com/r/Iceland/comments/2e3ijf/gigantic_marshmallows_on_icelandic_farms.

Gudmundsson, Bjarni. "Hay Drying in Iceland." ScytheConnection. July 24, 2013. http://scytheconnection.com/hay-drying-in-iceland.

Hanson, Curtis, and Jennifer Joe. "Marshmallow Fields." TravelBlog. September 20, 2015. www.travelblog.org/Europe/Iceland/Northwest/Snaefellsnes/blog-900360.html.

"How Do They Make Marshmallows?" HowStuffWorks. April 1, 2000. http://recipes.howstuffworks.com/question128.htm.

Iceland in Pictures. June 7, 2011. http://icelandinpictures.com/post/6280727010/summercamp-kids-art-icelandic-farm.

Ishida, Aki. Iceland in June. July 3, 2013. http://icelandinjune.tumblr.com/post/54550334259/andhere-in-iceland-marshmallows-are-grown-in.

Jonsson, Jodi. "Marshmallow Farm in Iceland!" Lost in Iceland. Pinterest. Accessed May 17, 2017. www.pinterest.com/pin/359021401516545229.

Long, Matt. "31 Weird Facts about Iceland That Will Amaze You." LandLopers. June 22, 2015. https://landlopers.com/2015/06/21/facts-about-iceland.

Matthíasson, Björn, and Valdimar Kristinsson. "Iceland." *Encyclopædia Britannica*. April 5, 2017. www.britannica.com/place/Iceland.

"Reykjavik, Iceland—Sunrise, Sunset, and Daylength, January 2017." Timeanddate.com. Accessed May 17, 2017. www.timeanddate.com/sun/iceland/reykjavik?month=1.

Here, Hyena-Hyena-Hyena!

Allison, Simon. "A Close Encounter of the Wild Kind: The Hyena Men of Harar." *Daily Maverick*. August 7, 2015. www.dailymaverick.co.za/article/2015-08-07-a-close-encounter-of-wild-kind-the-hyena-men-of-harar#.WRxjpFKZOgR.

Autin, Beth. "Spotted Hyena (*Crocuta Crocuta*) Fact Sheet, 2014. Population & Conservation Status." ResearchGuides at International Environment Library Consortium. 2014. http://ielc.libguides.com/sdzg/factsheets/spottedhyena/population.

Baynes-Rock, Marcus. "Hyenas in Harar." August 9, 2016. https://hararhyenas.wordpress.com.

Bhalla, Nita. "Africa | The Hyena Man of Harar." BBC News. July 1, 2002. http://news.bbc.co.uk/2/hi/africa/2079781.stm.

Choat, Isabel. "Planet Earth II: The Most Amazing Places, Chosen by Producers." *Guardian*. November 8, 2016. www.theguardian.com/travel/2016/nov/08/planet-earth-ii-david-attenborough-bbc-amazing-places.

Fletcher, Martin. "The Urban Hyenas That Attack Rough Sleepers." BBC News. February 23, 2014. www.bbc.com/news/magazine-26294631.

J-U, Lily. "Notes from Kenya: MSU Hyena Research." Urban Hyenas in Ethiopia. February 9, 2017. http://msuhyenas.blogspot.com/2017/02/urban-hyenas-in-ethiopia.html.

Linthicum, Kate. "Ethiopia Hyenas: Not Biting the Hand That Feeds Them." *Los Angeles Times*. July 31, 2010. http://articles.latimes.com/2010/jul/31/world/la-fg-harar-hyenas-20100731.

Lorentz, Michael. "The Hyena Man of Harar." Africa Geographic. March 22, 2016. https://africageographic.com/blog/hyena-man-harar.

Murdock, Heather. "Hyenas Not a Laughing Matter in Ethiopia." *Washington Times*. June 30, 2010. www.washingtontimes.com/news/2010/jun/30/hyenas-not-a-laughing-matter-in-ethiopia.

"Spotted Hyena." *National Geographic*. Accessed May 18, 2017. www.nationalgeographic.com/animals/mammals/s/spotted-hyena.

Stratton, Mark. "Ethiopia: The Hyena Men of Harar." *National Geographic Traveller.* May 6, 2015. www.natgeotraveller.co.uk/destinations/africa/ethiopia/the-hyena-men-of-harar.

PHOTOGRAPH CREDITS

The authors would like to thank the following for granting permission to reproduce the images used in this book:

page 1 © aphotostory/Shutterstock
page 2 National Park Service Digital Image Archives/Wikimedia Commons
page 3 Daniel Shwen/Wikimedia
page 4 © I David Keith Jones/images of Africa Photobank/Alamy Stock Photo
page 6 LCpl Chloe Nelson, United States Marine Corps/Wikimedia Commons
page 7 adam_jones/Flickr
page 8 Stefano Benazzi/American Journal of Physical Anthropology
page 11 mapswire.com
page 12–13 Marie-Lan Nguyen/Wikimedia Commons
page 14 © Chronicle/Alamy Stock Photo
page 16 G. Elliot Smith, Catalogue General Antiquites Egyptiennes du Musee du Caire: The Royal Mummies, The University of Chicago Libraries/Wikimedia Commons
page 17 Peter Pelham/Wellcome Library no. 6370i
page 18 © MPI/Archive Photos/Getty Images
page 20 James Gathany/Centers for Disease Control and Prevention's Public Health Image Library
page 21 Iridescent/Wikimedia Commons
page 22 © Science & Society Picture Library/Getty Images
page 23 Jappalang/Wikimedia Commons
page 25 © Heritage Image Partnership Ltd/Alamy Stock Photo
page 27 Used with permission of Paul Guinan and Anina Bennett
page 28 (both) Used with permission of Paul Guinan and Anina Bennett
page 31 John Syme/The White House Historical Association/Wikimedia Commons
page 32 John James Audubon/Wikimedia Commons
page 33 Smithsonian Institution Archives, Image #SIA2012-6089
page 36 Lilpop,Rau&Loewenstein/Wikimedia Commons
page 38 book cover art © Joana Kruse/Alamy Stock Photo
page 40 Courtesy of Sears Brands, LLC
page 41 Air-force-NORAD file photo Wikimedia Commons
page 42 Michael Kucharek/NORAD (The appearance of U.S. Department of Defense (DoD) visual information does not imply or constitute DoD endorsement.)
page 45 © Andrey_Kuzmin/Shutterstock
page 46 Arkyan/Wikimedia Commons
page 47 © Sammy Yuen
page 48–49 Pseudopanax/Wikimedia Commons
page 50 Boston Public Library Tichnor Brothers collection #91445/Wikimedia Commons

page 51 © Dr. Robert E. Bailey

page 52 (top) © Dr. Robert E. Bailey; (bottom) Boston Public Library Tichnor Brothers collection #91424/ Wikimedia Commons

page 53 (top) Boston Public Library Tichnor Brothers collection #91446/Wikimedia Commons; (bottom) Boston Public Library Tichnor Brothers collection #91113/Wikimedia Commons

page 55 JJ Harrison (jjharrison89@facebook.com)/Wikimedia Commons

page 56–57 © Vincent Kessler/Reuters

page 58 © Vincent Kessler/Reuters

page 61 Kevin Baugh/Wikimedia Commons

page 62 Kevin Baugh/Wikimedia Commons

page 64 United States Central Intelligence Agency's World Factbook/Wikimedia Commons

page 65 © satriaangga7/iStockPhoto LP

page 66 Flickr/Matt Smith

page 68 Petr Kratochvil/PublicDomainPictures.net

page 69 © Sira Anamwong/Shutterstock

page 70 Martin Tajmr (mtajmr)/Pixabay

page 71 © Sammy Yuen

page 74 © Thomas Peter/Reuters

page 75 © Elaine Kurtenbach/Associated Press

page 76 © Thomas Peter/Reuters

page 79 © HistoricCamera.com

page 80 © NMPFT/SSPL/The Image Works

page 81 The Strand Magazine/The Arthur Conan Doyle Encyclopedia

page 84–85 Dun.can (duncanh1)/Flickr

page 86 London Evening Standard, 19 Oct 1970. Photo: © David Farrant

page 89 © Image Source Trading Ltd/Shutterstock

page 90 Joseph Duplessis, National Portrait Gallery/Wikimedia Commons

page 91 Benjamin West, Philadelphia Museum of Art/Wikimedia Commons

page 92 Laurie Ann Thompson

page 95 © Edmund Terakopian/PA Images/Alamy Stock Photo

page 96 moaksey/Flickr

page 97 David Rydevik/Wikimedia Commons

page 98 Cantus/Wikimedia Commons

page 100 © princigalli/iStockPhoto LP

page 101 Tech. Sgt. J.T. May III/U.S. Air Force

page 103 Zureks/Wikimedia Commons

page 106 Courtesy of Amber Langerud Photography

page 107 Courtesy of Lakes Country Connection

page 109 NordNordWest/Wikimedia Commons

page 110 © Asad Zia

page 112 © Asad Zia

page 113 © kurhan/Shutterstock

page 114 Alan and Jeanne Abel

page 115 Randy Robertson/Flickr

page 116 Vmenkov/Wikimedia Commons

page 119 © Heino Kalis/Reuters

page 120 (map) NordNordWest/Wikimedia Commons; (bottom) Graham McLellan (gforce)/Flickr

page 121 Łukasz Lech (gibffe)/Flickr

INDEX

Page numbers in *italics* refer to illustrations.

Audubon, John James
    The Birds of America by, 31–32
    fake species by, *33*, 33–34, *34*
    prank by, 32–35
    as wildlife artist, 31, *31*
automaton. *See* robots

banyan
    arrest and verdict of, 111–12
    as criminal, 109–12
    in Landi Kotal, 109, 112
Barrett, Judi and Ron, 115–16, 144
Bath, Britain, 11, *11*
bathers
    curse on thieving, 10, 12–13, *13*
    irate, 12
    revered place for, 11
    valuables left by, 12–13
Baugh, Kevin, 60–63, *61*, *62*
Baughston, Molossia, 62
bees, *55*
    honey production from, 55–59, *58*
    honey stomachs in, 56
    M&M's used by, 56–57
    waste influencing, 56–59
Bennett, Anina, 27, 138
big-mouth sucker (*Catostomus megastomus*), 33
biohazard, 38
biomagnetism, 102–3, 143
Bird Brain booth, 54
The Birds of America (Audubon), 31–32
Bitumen, 9
black buffalo-fish (*Catostomus niger*), 33
Boilerplate, 138
    Campion brainchild of, 27
    classified mission for, 28–29
    conspiracy theories concerning, 29
    famous admirers of, 30
Boilerplate: History's Mechanical Marvel (Guinan and Bennett), 27, 138
bona fide, 100, 101

Franklin, Benjamin
    on farts, 91–94
    as revolutionary and politician, *90*, 90–91, *91*
    satire of, 92–94
Frieh, Alain, 57–58

games, fact or fake, 43, 139
geography, 45
geological wonders, fact or fake, 49, 140
Gerbillus leonurus (lion-tail jumping mouse), 34
gereja ayam. *See* chicken church
ghosts. *See* specter
ghost ship. *See* ships
goddess
    Minerva as, 12
    worship of, 12–13
Google, 133
gravestone inscriptions, fact or fake, 24, 138
Great Pyrenees, *106*, 107, *107*
guano, 3
Guinan, Paul, 27, 138

Hanover, Rex, 38
Harar, Ethiopia
    hyena men of, 127, 128–30, *130*
    hyenas in, *127*, 127–30, *128*, *130*
    visitors to, 129–30
hay
    combine for, 124, 125
    as fodder, 124–25
    for marshmallows, *124–25*, 124–26
hero, Smith as, 95, 96–98
Highgate Cemetery
    catacombs in, 83, 84
    history of, 83–84, *84–85*, 87–88
    mausoleums in, 83, 84
    preserving of, *84–85*, 87–88
    vampires at, *86*, 86–87
history, 1
    comparing of, 131

North American Aerospace Defense Command (NORAD), 40–41
    Santa tracked by, 42–44
    technologies at, 42–43

obsession, 5
occult, 85
Ohio red-eye (*Aplocentrus calliops*), 33
ominous, 96
Onesimus, 17, 18, 20

Pakistan, 109, *109*, 112
passion, 5
Peng, Jessica, 66–67
petition, 62
photos. *See* images
Phuket, Thailand, 95
placard, 112
play-people, 77
porridge, 129
postmortem, 25
post office, 14
poxy, 10
precarious, 4, 5
predecessor, 41
Price, Richard, 93
Prout, G. Clifford, 113, *113*, *114*
proverb, 91
psychologist
    Brelands as, 51, *51*, 53–54
    on rats, 38

Rafinesque, Constantine, 32–35
Railway of the Dead. *See* London Necropolis Railway
Ramses V (pharaoh), 16, *16*
rats, 139
    as biohazard, 38
    as cannibals, 38, *38*, 39
    potential paradise for, 37
refurbishing, 76
repercussions, tsunami, 96, *97*, 98

READ THE SERIES

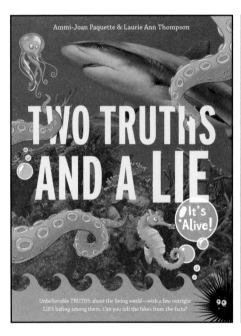

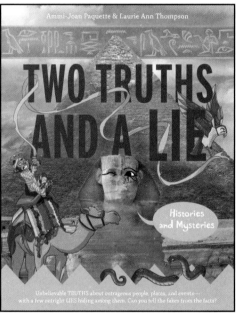

WALDEN POND PRESS™
An Imprint of HarperCollins*Publishers*

www.walden.com/books • www.harpercollinschildrens.com

More Must-Read
Books from
Walden Pond Press

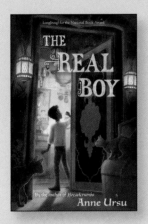

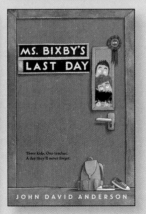

Also available as ebooks.